THE ENGLISH COUNTRY CHAIR

An Illustrated History of Chairs
and
Chairmaking

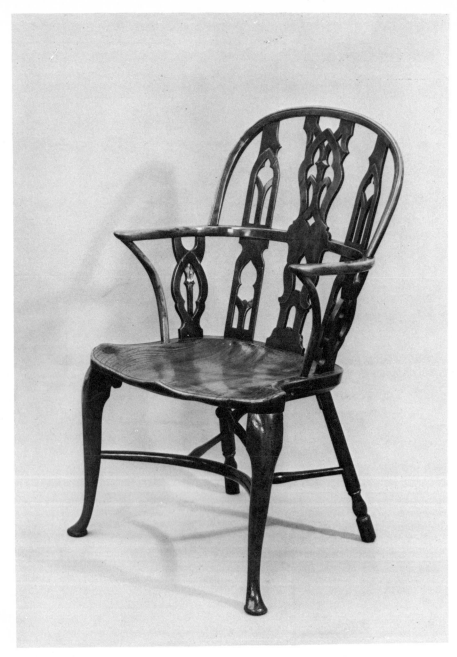

The Windsor Chair of the 1760's

THE ENGLISH COUNTRY CHAIR

An illustrated history of chairs and chairmaking

IVAN G. SPARKES

SPURBOOKS LIMITED

Published by Spurbooks Ltd.
6 Parade Court,
Bourne End, Buckinghamshire

I.S.B.N. 0 904978 87 7

Second, revised edition 1977

Printed in Great Britain by
Chapel River Press, Andover, Hants.

CONTENTS

LIST OF ILLUSTRATIONS

INTRODUCTION

The background to the English chair, its design, history and especially the life of the people who made it, presents a fascinating story to those who care to seek it. In writing this volume I have found myself leaning heavily on the books, articles and notes of many other researchers to whom I owe a debt of gratitude. Most of their names appear in the list of sources printed at the end of this book, but in particular the work of John Gloag, Edward T. Joy and L. J. Mayes should be mentioned, who have researched deeply on both the national and the local scene, adding considerably to our knowledge of the history of the chair, and the chairmaking industry.

This does not profess to be a technical book, nor can it claim to be a design survey, but I hope in reading these pages, something of what Frank Hudson calls 'the excited interest you always get if you are in a craft trade' will show through and add a few more adherents to the study of the English Chair.

The photographs are reproduced by courtesy of The Design Centre, The Victoria and Albert Museum, The Parker-Knoll Collection, The Council for Industrial Design, The Museum of English Rural Life, The Wycombe Chair Museum, High Wycombe, Mr. E. Sweetland, The Henry Francis du Pont Winterthur Museum and The American Museum, Bath.

Part One: Craft and Industry

Chapter One

UNDER THE BEECHWOOD TREE

'When I began this trade' said a chairmaker in the 1860's, 'I loaded a cart and travelled to Luton.' All there was prosperous. There was a scramble for my chairs, and when I came home I laid my receipts on my table and said to my wife 'You never saw so much money before'. This recollection takes us back to the beginning of the nineteenth century, when the chair industry in towns such as High Wycombe in the Chilterns was in its infancy. Back to a time when factories were virtually unknown and when most chairs were made piecemeal, partly in the woods and partly in cottage workshops.

The forests were the natural places for woodturners, for there, among the lovely beeches of the Chilterns, with unlimited timber around them and the tools of the wheelwright and rakemaker in their hands, the rural crafts flourished. Here skills and techniques were handed down from father to son, from master to apprentice, ensuring in later years sufficient trained craftsmen to transform this active cottage craft into a thriving industry.

The background of these chairmakers, or 'bodgers' as they have become known, has often been over-romanticised by the magazine writers. A craft cult arose just prior to and following the Second World War, when it was realised that this breed of rural craftsmen was dying out. Putting much of the fantasy aside, there emerges a canny, hardworking and skilful artisan who could whittle a chair leg out of a sliver of beechwood and make a type of chair which is now finding its true place in the world of antique furniture.

When did this cottage industry commence? It is not always realised that chairs were not added to the range of domestic furniture until Elizabethan times. Before then, particularly in medieval days, it was only the Lord of the Manor or some such important person who owned and used an armchair. These were then known as 'chairs of estate' and except in the case of noble households, only one would be in evidence. This would often be placed in a prominent position, usually against a wall in the hall with a 'cloth of state' or heraldic tapestry hanging behind it, and, as the chair was very heavy, it was seldom moved.

13

The Coronation Chair in Westminster Abbey, upon which all English Kings have been crowned since the 13th century, is a fine example of the joyned chair, and was made about 1296.

An oak 'joyned' stool dated about 1600. This was the main form of seating up to the 16th century.

The famous Coronation Chair in Westminster Abbey, one of the few to survive, is perhaps the oldest English 'joyned' chair in existence. It was made by Walter of Durham about 1296, when the Stone of Scone upon which the Scottish Kings were crowned was brought from Scotland and incorporated in the seat. As with other medieval furniture, the chair was originally brightly coloured and gilded in a decoration carried out by the King's painter. The style is typical of many other chairs which are illustrated in the manuscripts and paintings of the medieval period.

These early chairs were made by carpenters or wheelwrights and the Guild of Joyners had existed in London since 1309, but it was not until the seventeenth century that the craft of chairmaking as such, was fully recognised and recorded. An early reference is found in a record of 1622 at the Norwich City Archives in the list of those 'Borne of Parents Strangers inhabitinge in the County and Citty of Norwich'. Here are given the names of two *'chayremakers'* – Abraham Lanes and Mordoche Ffromettell. As their parents were listed as 'Strangers' to Norwich, it is possible that they may have originally come from London. For there, since the mid-sixteenth century, a colony of furniture makers had resided

A very fine unusual oak back chair of the 17th century, carved with the arms of Thomas Wentworth, 1st Earl of Stratford.

and worked in the area between the Tower of London and St. Paul's Cathedral. As early as 1584, Edward Philip is recorded as owning an upholstery shop in Cornhill.

The bench or joyned stool was the most commonly used form of seating up to the sixteenth century, particularly in the dining room where they were often made to match the table and other furniture. These were made in a framework of thick oak rails and heavily turned legs which were secured by pegs or dowels. This was topped by a seat of thick planks forming a sturdy stool which could take rough treatment. During later Elizabethan times, the legs lost some of their earlier heaviness and were splayed outwards to give them stability. At some point these stools were given framed or solid wooden backs and were called *backstools*. This would be the type of seats mentioned in the Shirley Inventory of 1620 from Faringdon in Berkshire, which refers to 'a stoole with a back; two chayres and one back chaier'. In order that the true dignity of the armchair owners should not be slighted, these new chairs were not treated as real chairs, but were called backstools up to at least 1760. Another chair which afforded its owner great status was the continental X-shape, which in the sixteenth century was the prerogative of royalty. Usually it was well upholstered, and in the seventeenth century was still used chiefly in the wealthier households. A form known as the 'Glastonbury Chair' became linked with ecclesiastical furniture in the late sixteenth century and developed into the folding chair.

To meet the problem of the enormous hooped dresses of the period, a very wide upholstered chair was produced. This became known as the 'farthingale chair' after the name given to the framework used to make the heavily decorated skirts stand out from the body in the accepted fashion. Originally the farthingale was a Spanish style, and the whalebone hoop was a hazard when a lady attempted to sit down. To use an armchair would be to court disaster, but a wide backstool allowed the great hoop to rest gracefully with the dress draperies flowing to the ground. As the contemporary ballad records,

'They brought in fashions strange and new,
With golden garments bright.
The farthingale, and mighty ruffles,
With gownes of rare delight.'

During the same period the three-legged stools were being developed into chairs with a triangular seat, known as bobbin-frame or thrown chairs. Made with turned backs and framework, they were heavily decorated with spindles and bobbins, so much so that one writer felt they

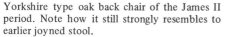

Yorkshire type oak back chair of the James II period. Note how it still strongly resembles to earlier joyned stool.

An oak Farthingale chair c.1684 with later upholstery, made to accommodate the large hooped dress worn at the courts.

represented a frenzy of turnery which had no parallel on the continent. Most surviving examples of the bobbin-frame chair are seventeenth century, although the style was certainly known in the sixteenth century. They seem to have been made chiefly in Wales, the Severn Valley, Cheshire and Lancashire.

Such chairs were for the gentlefolk, and seldom were found in the homes of the yeoman farmer or cottager. About this time the situation began to change, and the Restoration of Charles the Second in 1660 saw the introduction into England of crafts and furnishing materials which had been denied the population during the Commonwealth Period. A petition of the 1680's draws attention to the fact that 'about 1664, cane-chairs came into use in England, which gave so much satisfaction to all the Nobility, Gentry and Commonality of this Kingdom (for their durableness, lightness and cleanliness from dust, worms, and moths) that they came to be used in England and sent to all parts of the world'. The Great Fire of London of 1666 caused terrible destruction of houses and furniture, and the need for replacements revived the industry con-

The Queen Anne influence is shown in the back of this unusual Windsor chair dated c.1720. *(Parker-Knoll Collection)*

Restoration cane armchair c.1680 in walnut with the seat and back panels in canework.

siderably. The cane-chair makers came over from the Continent, in particular from Holland, and the Hugenots followed after 1685, bringing with them their skill in weaving to create new materials and patterns for the chair and upholstery industry of London.

These new cane chairs with their elegance and lightness were in great contrast to the much more solid furniture of Cromwellian days. The introduction of a raked back also made for greater comfort and the increased use of elaborate carving produced a chair which had the rival upholsterers worried. The petition mentioned above begged Parliament to prohibit their production in this country, but the Bill was not passed. In 1689 another petition was drawn up on behalf of the people of Bedford and referred to a Parliamentary Committee because 'since cane chairs have been in Use, the Trade hath decayed, and is lost, now the said Poor, that used to be employed, beg their bread; and the Town, and others near it, without some Redress, will come to Ruin'.

When an inventory was made of the goods of Richard Brown, a yeoman of Writtle in the year 1713, it was recorded that there were 'seven rush bottomed chairs in the kitchen, twelve cane chairs in the parlour, four joynt stools and six leather chairs in the Hall.' In other rooms in the farmhouse were 'six black chairs, eleven red chairs and a number of old chairs'. This represents an unusually large number of chairs for the period, and if this is an example of other houses in the country, one can realise why the upholsterers were worried.

The peak of the cane chair was about 1694, after which time it went out of fashion and by 1740 was hardly ever made until introduced once again with great success in Victorian days.

Fashionable chairs were mainly obtainable in London, and the towns in the provinces, for the people in the heart of the countryside still relied for the most part on locally made items. Very few early rural chairs survive to this day, for they were not fine chairs which were prized, but practical pieces of furniture which were heavily used. Some seem to be prototypes of later designs, such as the remarkable fifteenth century three-legged chair which is recorded as being preserved at St. Cross Hospital near Winchester. This seems to be an obvious forerunner of the low back Windsor chair with legs and spindles shaped by spokeshaves, while the curved arms and solid U-shaped seat strongly resembles the smoker's bow of the late nineteenth century. Another is the unusual 'Queen Anné' type Windsor in the Parker-Knoll Collection, dated as c.1720. Although the legs of this chair have been cut down, they still show a rough attempt at the cabriole leg which was a feature of the finer type of eighteenth century Windsor chair.

In the Georgian period, particularly with the rise of the Whigs, new policies of commerce and colonial trading led to increased prosperity. In 1727 John Brown, Chairmaker and Cabinet maker at the 'Three Cover'd Chair and Walnut Tree' in London made 'All sorts of Windsor Garden Chairs of all sizes painted green or in the wood'. The merchants became landowners and wanted to spend lavishly in order to show their new status. Jane Austen's description of Sir William Lucas in her novel 'Pride and Prejudice' published in 1813, is very apt, for he 'had been formerly in trade in Meryton, where he had made a tolerable fortune, and risen to the honour of knighthood by an address to the king during his mayoralty'. 'The distinction had, perhaps, been felt too strongly. It had given him a disgust for his business and to his residence in a small market town; and quitting them both, he had removed with his family to a house about a mile from Meryton, denominated from that period Lucas Lodge; where he could think with pleasure of his own importance'.

The most popular form of the Windsor chair has been the wheel back, in which the splat is pierced with the design of a wheel with six spokes. This pattern became common about 1820-30.

The Gothic revival of the 1750's, connected with Horace Walpole (1717-1797) promoted an equal interest in Gothic style decoration so that designers such as Chippendale could produce drawings of chairs, which, after being made up in London out of mahogany for the Gentry, were copied in yew, beech and elm as Windsor chairs for the rural folk. Although the cities had their place in social life, England was still chiefly a country of villages, and in the rural society so typically illustrated in the novels of Jane Austen, the furniture used by all within it was often made locally. So this is where the rural chair, often the Windsor or ladder-back chair came into its own.

Although the Windsor chair is chiefly linked with the Chilterns, it was also produced in a number of other areas, including Norfolk, Lancashire, North Wales and the West Country. The last two centres were probably developed from Bristol which was the important manufacturing town of the West. The reason for the industry settling in Buckinghamshire was mainly due to the large areas of forest in which the beech tree grew so abundantly. Daniel Defoe (1660-1731) author of 'Robinson Crusoe' writing in 1725, states in his 'Tour' that 'a vast quantity of Beechwood, which grows in the woods of Buckinghamshire more plentifully than in any other part of England' provided 'beech quarters for divers uses, particularly chair makers and turnery wares'. 'The quantity of this brought down from hence is almost incredible, yet so is the country overgrown with the beech in these parts that it is bought very reasonable, nor is there likely to be any scarcity of it for time to come'.

The popularity of the Windsor over other rural chairs is shown in Loudon's Encyclopedia of 1833 when he writes that it was 'one of the best kitchen chairs in general use in the Midland counties of England'. This type of chair is for most people the familiar wheelback, but that pattern is only one out of a number of styles. Although the wheel motif dates back to the 1820's, it was preceded in the early eighteenth century by the comb-back and fan-back which were very popular until the 1750's when the hoop-back, or as it is more usually called the bow-back, came into vogue.

For the first mention of a Windsor chair, we must cross the Atlantic Ocean to Colonial America. When John Jones, a merchant of Philadelphia died in 1708, among the inventory of his goods, clothing and furniture are listed three Windsor chairs. It is interesting to conjecture whether these chairs came across from England when he or his family emigrated. Certainly it was common practice for Colonists to take some basic pieces of furniture when they sailed to the New World. As Philadelphia became the centre for early Windsors, these chairs may well have formed the pattern for the Colonial style Windsor chairs which have developed independently in the United States of America.

In England, the Windsor chair is chiefly confined to the cottage or the servants' quarters. Even up to the twentieth century, when it is again widely manufactured, the style has been created primarily for the kitchen, nursery, dining room or school. In the past it figured largely in the tavern or club. Of all the clubs in the nineteenth century, few are more familiar to us than that famous group in fiction, created by Charles Dickens, called the Pickwick Club. It is in Robert Seymour's jovial plate of the 1836 in which Mr. Pickwick addresses the club that we see the Windsor chair so véry much at home. Indeed it appears in a number of Dickens' novels, although more often pictured in poor or lower class settings. Trollope also featured it in 'The Last Chronicle of Barset' where Mr. Crawley's house is described as having a 'wretched, poverty stricken room, with a Windsor chair as such used to be called, made soft by an old cushion in the back'.

So far the Windsor chair has appeared as a well known friend, but at some point the question must arise as to precisely how it differs in construction from other chairs. As mentioned earlier, chairs have developed from the bench or stool, and in time the timbers of the back legs were extended up past the seat to form back supports to take a panel or rail, and this was known as the back chair or back stool. A quick glance at most dining room chairs, especially if based on eighteenth century models will show this feature. With the Windsor chair, the stool still forms the basic design, with the back and the arms socketed into the seat from above, and the legs socketed into it from below. In this way the back legs and back supports of the Windsor can *never,* as with other styles, be made of one continuous piece of wood, and no matter how the design varies, in the shape of the legs, the back, or with the use of a solid or caned seat, a glance at the back legs will soon confirm its true nature.

It would be wrong to think that the Windsor chair was totally banished from the drawing room and never appeared above stairs in its heyday. The Duke of Chandos had seven japanned Windsor chairs in his library at Cannons in 1725, while Lord Percival, when visiting Hall Barn in Buckinghamshire in 1724, saw his wife 'carryd in a Windsor chair' around the many winding walks in the gardens there, causing me to wonder if she sat in one of the so-called Garden Machines or invalid chairs which were advertised in William Webb's trade card of c.1792.

So the Windsor chair has, like the donkey, had its day, but the origin of the name is still uncertain. The most popular meaning stems from the story which describes how George III was caught in a rainstorm near Windsor. Taking refuge in a cottage, His Highness sat on the best chair in the room and being well pleased with its comfort, required similar ones to be made for Windsor Castle. Unfortunately for this theory, the style existed and was so called long before the Georges came to the throne of England!

Another theory refers to the time when Edward, third Lord Windsor, entertained Queen Elizabeth I at Bradenham, only a few miles out of High Wycombe whilst on one of her many perambulations around the English countryside. It is known that the Windsor Family held this manor for many years up to 1642, but the link is rather tenuous, and there are no references to the chair by this name as early as the first quarter of the seventeenth century.

In the end I find myself agreeing with those writers who connect the origin of the name with the manufacture and sale of these chairs to the London dealers at the Windsor Market and along the main road from Windsor to London. For one can imagine the London chair dealers, used as they were to the finer mahogany and walnut products of the London workshops, referring in a derogatory way to the latest batch of beech chairs 'up from Windsor'.

Chapter Two

THE BODGER IN THE WOODS

Over two hundred years ago, Daniel Defoe described the Chilterns as having a vast quantity of beechwood, adding 'nor is there likely to be a scarcity of it for time to come'. In this he was prophetic, for even now, as a recent census of woodlands have shown, the Chilterns has still the largest acreage of beech high forest of all English counties.

This was not the result of proper planning in the past, for even if the beech was the life-blood of the nineteenth century chairmaker, scientific tree renewal didn't come high on his list of priorities. Timber merchants objected to the use of planted beeches, much preferring the age-old custom of allowing the nuts to fall from the trees and germinate in their own way. It was however quite usual to thin out some of the timber in rotation to allow light to reach the growing trees. This was vital as the beech grows close together, and they will draw each other up to the sun. It was also necessary to fell the heavy topped trees and so create the proper spacing of the crowns of foliage. Such practices date back to the seventeenth century, for Dr. Robert Plot (1640-96) writing in 1677 and referring to the Chilterns, noted that the owners did not sell whole sections of the forest for timber, but instead they would 'draw them almost every year according as their wood come to be fit scantling'. We can sympathise with the poetic outcry of Thomas Campbell (1777-1844) in his 'Beech tree's petition'.

> O leave this barren spot to me!
> Spare woodman, spare the beechen tree!

But the beech has long been a source of revenue for the estate owners in this area, as timber grown on a heavy soil which overlies chalk has a reputation for strength and durability. Another useful quality of beech is the straightness of its timber and closeness of grain. This makes beechwood tough, difficult to split and easy to match in jointing. To enhance these qualities, in some districts whole plantations were stooled or cut back close to the roots. This ensured that the new shoots grew in clusters of straight twigs which matured into useful straight poles. Although this straightness of grain gives beech added flexibility so that it

24

will bend easily, the tree does not make old bones, and is more suitable for indoor rather than outdoor use.

The felling of the trees took place in the autumn and winter months when the sap is down. The timber was usually sold felled, and the purchaser allowed a year in which to make arrangements for its removal. When a fall or stand of beech was put up for auction, it sold in loads of 40 cubic feet, the number of trees in a load varying in relation to the size of the trees. Those of small girth were sometimes sold at from sixpence to ninepence a cubic foot, while trees with a large quarter girth were known to reach half-a-crown a cubic foot. The average price in 1900 was from one shilling to one shilling and sixpence a cubic foot. In 1909 a load would sell for thirty-six shillings. In 1914 an average load is given as 25 cubic feet and the going rate for felling was one shilling a load.

The trees were selected and marked with a scratcher by the agent to ensure that no mistake was made in the felling. Trees from small to medium girth were preferred to large trees for making the chair legs. Beech can be described as red or male beech or white or female beech; red beech was said to be more esteemed, but this may well have been a pun, for it was apparently only the steamed wood of the beech tree.

The canniness of the woodsmen is apparent in their treatment of the Londoner. In Stokenchurch, a village which lies on the Oxford Road about ten miles west of High Wycombe, it seems that the measuring rule varied from the standard. Whereas he bought timber at the local rate of 37 inches to the yard, the local timber merchant had no hesitation in selling to the Government Agents at the imperial yard of 36 inches, thus ensuring a more adequate profit margin in the process.

Sometimes the felling was done by the vendor's woodsmen, but often this was done by the Bodgers themselves. Samuel Rockell, a bodger of Naphill, recalls the man who helped him with this task, who had recently retired at the age of eighty! He commented what a wonderful old man he was 'to do as he did at so great an age'. Samuel had difficulty in getting anyone else to help him in the felling. This scarcity of labour is not reflected in the picture drawn by Peter Kalm in 1748 when 'a number of labourers were engaged in wood cutting. The chips which resulted were not left strewn around the hill, but it was the duty of one of the carts to gather them together and lay them in heaps.' Very little waste was allowed in the felling. The top and lop, as the smaller branches were called, was trimmed off with a siding up axe and sold for kindling faggots. The mast or bushwood from the beach and oak was gathered to be used as food for pigs, but the acorns had to lie a while in case they harmed the swine.

The chair bodgers worked in the beech woods of the Chilterns, making the legs for the Windsor chairs.

In the late eighteenth century even the remaining part of the trunk and roots were dug out and cut into small pieces and arranged into heaps to dry. The use of coal was not common in the country until late in the nineteenth century, as plenty of fuel was available in the woods. Beech faggots were also used by charcoal burners, and although the craft is no longer practiced today, charcoal for the blacksmith's forge and the metalsmelter's fire was once a normal sight, as it was prepared in the woods.

At this point the timber was cut into planks by sawing lengthwise along the trunk for use in making the chair seats, or sawn crossways into logs to be split by the bodger when making his chair legs. This term 'bodger' is given to the wood turner who makes the legs and stretchers which form the under frame of the chair. Its origin is uncertain and it may not have been in common use until the present century. It is possibly the name used by the London chairmakers or the Wycombe paper makers when referring to the rough conditions under which the leg-turners laboured. An interesting definition in the Oxford English Dictionary suggests that the word is a corruption of badger, which was a travelling pedlar. As some chair bodgers worked in pairs and travelled around, working in the woods where the timber was available and selling their turned wares at the best price they could get, this meaning is quite feasible. The Germans also have a word which is rather similarly used to describe a cooper, the word is *bottcher;* while as late as 1938 a union magazine in Wycombe uses the term bojjer instead of the more accepted spelling.

The sawing of the tree trunk into planks was a very laborious task, and was still done by hand until well into the twentieth century, the men working over a sawpit. These pits were often permanent affairs, about as deep as a man's height and up to fifteen feet in length. In the woodland clearings a temporary pit would be dug and two logs laid along the top with two shorter ones across each end. These logs, which supported the timber being sawn into planks, were called the 'strakes' and 'sills'. The pit sawyers worked in pairs, and it was the duty of the second man to dig and prepare the pit, a herculean task in itself. The first man's responsibility was the upkeep of the saw and the preparation of the timber for sawing. He was the senior man, the Gaffer, and he usually owned the saw and arranged the work.

The tree trunk was at first hewn roughly flat on the upper and lower surfaces to help keep it level when placed in position over the pit. It was then secured by iron dogs or spikes to the sills and strakes. Guide-lines were marked in either charcoal or chalk on the timber with the help of a taut piece of cord to show the sawing position. The first cut was made dead in the middle of the trunk; this was called 'splitting the heart'. It was felt that this initial cut stopped ring-shake which might occur when the annular rings of the timber shake and separate from the older heart of the tree.

The saw which was used was extremely large, over seven feet in length and tapered in width from about ten inches at the top to three inches at the bottom. This tapering helped in the movement of the saw in the wood and reduced the bottom weight making it easier for the lower pit-sawyer to return it to the 'up' position. The handles of the saw were detachable, for the blade had to be slid out of each saw-cut as work proceeded down the trunk. The handle at the top was most suitably called the tiller, for it guided the saw. The handle in the pit was termed the box.

The saw was steered by the top man, and it was in the down stroke that the cutting was done. The man underneath was responsible for pushing the blade back up and all the sawdust showered down upon him. His was a most unhappy lot, for beside the problem of the sawdust, his view was obscured by the mass of timber above him. He also had the task of

The timber being sawn into planks over the saw-pit. The head of the lower pitman can just be seen between the timbers, as the man above steers the saw along its path.

periodically oiling the saw blade with a piece of oily rag stuck on a stick, to make the saw move easily. To top it all, in the winter months the light could be so bad that he needed a candle stuck in a recess in the pit to enable him to see at all.

The plank widths were each cut in turn, and sawn one by one outwards from the centre cut for a part of the length of the timber, and then the trunk was levered forward to allow further sawing to recommence. To stop the sawn parts of the planks vibrating, a rope was thrown around the ends and tightened. This allowed the Gaffer to drive wedges into the saw-kerfs and so keep the path of the saw blade clear. So the continuous sawing up and down, with its accompanying sawdust, oil and sweat, proceeded until all the planks were cut and the trunk converted.

This form of sawing in the pit continued long after machinery had overtaken other functions in the timber trade. Indeed, the plank-sawing could often be the bottleneck in the woodyard. This delay in modernisation was possibly due to the difficulty in getting heavy machinery into the woods, and to the fact that until the bandsaw came into being, the circular saw could not be made large enough to cope with some of the larger trunks which the seven foot handsaw could easily handle. For what is often forgotten is that a circular saw can only cut up to half its diameter, and a truly gigantic one would be required to deal with the larger trees.

A report on the rural industries around Oxford, compiled by K. S. Woods in 1921, questioned the strength and durability of timber cut in the sawmills when compared with timber sawn in the woods. It also commented most unfavourably on the considerable damage the timber received when hauled by 'modern methods' over rough ground, a problem which did not arise with timbers dealt with on site.

At this point the bodger comes into the picture, for it was this problem of removing the trunks to a workshop which caused the chair bodgers to work in the woods. They usually worked in pairs, with the second man either a fellow worker or a lad learning the trade. Bodgers were not always their own masters, for in some instances they were employed by a local person, such as a farmer, and the chair-leg-turning was fitted in between other jobs on the land such as mowing, reaping and thatching, work which often took priority in the summer months.

One farmer in the Chilterns employed four men in the woods, producing chair legs and stretchers, at five shillings a gross for sale in High Wycombe and Stokenchurch factories.

When the bodgers bought a stand or fall of trees they would rig up their workshop among the trees. At first this would be an open hut with sloping sides meeting at the ridge and thatched with brushwood and bracken. The supports were saplings cut to twelve foot lengths and one tapered and tapped through a hole in the other about ten inches from the top. These were then opened out to about twelve foot at the ground and when side pieces joined the front and back frameworks together, it was ready for the bundles of brushwood to fill in the sloping walls. In later years, as tools and materials were more likely to be stolen, a wood and galvanised iron hut took its place, which could be locked when their daily stint was completed.

Life in the woods, according to George Dean, was 'strangely enjoyable . . . carefree, and a bit lonesome if your mate was away. In the spring it was lovely, as the trees took on their fresh green leaf and in the winter the sighing of the wind and the sight of the birds gathering in the branches when the smoke ascended at meal times'. As the camera shows, a most important task was the brewing of the tea. The sight of the kettle, suspended over the wood fire, or nestling among the glowing embers was the sign of bodgers at work, and it gave them extra incentive for a hard

The bodgers' hut was built among the trees and thatched with brushwood to keep out the bad weather. Much of the work was done in the open with the timber and finished chairlegs stacked in piles around the hut.

day's work. John Mayes, who visited some of the last of the bodgers in the woods around High Wycombe, speaks of the 'remarkable variety of tea with a wondrous smoky flavour about it'.

The two-handled cross-cut saw was used by the bodgers to cut the trunks into sections of chair leg length, and the sawhorses used had one pair of sloping legs to allow the heavy tree trunks to be edged gradually into position, propping them with pegs as they were levered inch by inch from the ground. It would be measured and marked off according to the type of leg required. The timber for the smoker's leg would need to be longer than that required for the leg of an ordinary Windsor bow. The resulting length of trunk would next be split into half and then again into quarters using an iron wedge and a beetle.

This beetle was a form of mallet used widely in rural woodwork. It was often heavier than a carpenter's mallet, barrel shaped and banded each end with metal rings. The quarters were placed on a low chopping block and with a sharp splitting out hatchet, were cleft into rough triangular pieces called billets. These must be cut most economically, for if they are too thick, extra time must be spent clearing away the spare wood, but if cut

Using a beetle and splitting out hatchet the log was split into half, quarters and finally into smaller pieces of wood called billets.

too thin, they would have to be rejected. From a section of trunk twelve inches in diameter it is possible to obtain about two dozen legs, with smaller size timbers the beetle was used with a *'froe'*, or *'fromard'* as it is sometimes called. This is a cutting tool in which the handle sits at right angles to the blade which has a lower cutting edge, a form of wedge used in several rural crafts.

The billets are next removed to a high chopping block, and with an angled short handled axe they are chopped more closely to a polygon or five sided shape and tapered at each end. The axe was ground on one side only, and was razor sharp. It was often fitted with a specially hardened steel tip inserted into the slip end of the blade by the local blacksmith.

The final shaping of the rough billet was completed on the shavehorse. This has a foot controlled vice in which the chair leg was clamped between the legs of the bodger who used a two-handled draw shave to smooth and prepare the billet for the pole lathe.

This lathe was based on one of the most primitive forms of turning, the principle of which was known as far back as Egyptian times, and due to its simplicity, was still in use as late as the early twentieth century. The pole

The polelathe in use, showing the chair leg with the cord which makes it revolve as the treadle is pressed, the chisels can be seen on the bench which are used in turning the pattern.

was very important in making up the lathe, and a real good one was a treasure. Care was taken to choose a young larch tree, grown to the right height and thickness. This was carefully peeled and often allowed to season for a while by lodging it in a handy tree. To make the pole springy it was shaved on the underside. When ready for use it was fixed just outside the workshop by a chain attached to a stout post driven into the ground. The other end of the pole was raised and passed through the eaves of the hut so that it was positioned directly over the spot where the lathe was to be set up. A piece of cord was dropped from the pole to the lathe, wound around the billet and passed down to the foot treadle. This billet was fixed between the head and tail stocks which are called poppets. The left hand side had a fixed mandrel and the right hand one was adjustable on a screwed rod to tighten up the work.

As the treadle was pressed down, the cord moved down also, causing the billet to revolve between the poppets and the pole to bend like a bow. When the treadle was released the pole sprang back into position, again rotating the wooden billet as it did so. When this simple action is speeded up and continually repeated, the chair leg turns at great speed and the bodger was then able to shave the spare wood away with a chisel as the billet rotated towards him.

A broad chisel was used first to remove the rough surface and create the round shape. The swells and rings, grooves and bevels were then marked with a pointed chisel, and using other gouges, such as the buz or V-shaped gouge, these decorations, or beads, as they are sometimes called, were firmly turned to the required pattern.

As each leg was completed, it was pushed through a hole in the side of the hut, and later stacked in piles through which the wind could blow. This enabled the green wood to dry and season a little before being sent to the factories for framing. The bodger sometimes had great difficulty in getting a good price for his wares. Mr. Hussey felt that 'some of the most cruelly treated in the chair trade years ago was these poor old wood turners doing their chairs like, out in the country. They'd bring a load into the town and try to sell them; well, some of the masters they wouldn't attempt to buy them not till they see they'd got to take them back home and they, well, knocked them down and get them cheap rather than drag them back home'.

The bodger, beside turning the actual chair legs, was expected to provide the three stretcher pieces which form the underframe of the chair. Before the Great War, he would receive five shillings for a gross, which would consist of a gross (144) chair legs and three-quarters of a gross (108) stretcher parts, making a total of over two hundred and fifty turned pieces. A man working from seven in the morning to seven at night for five and a half days a week could reckon to make two and a half gross per week and from this effort take home about twelve shillings a week to live on! The price per gross increased rapidly after 1914 until by 1920 it had risen to fourteen shillings.

The demand for hand turned legs continued for many years after machine turned legs were on the market. This was due to their superior quality, for the bodger split the timber along the grain, and he discarded pieces with bad knots. The War Office had for many years stipulated this

Chair-legs stacked to season.

type of leg in its contracts, but when it changed this part of the specification to allow machine made legs to be used, the death knell for the bodgers sounded through the Chilterns!

Over fifty years ago the Rural Industries Report forecast the end of the part the wood-turners played in chair production, stating that 'unless these turners can be enabled to find a better market on the strength of the superiority of hand-cleft legs and get favourable terms for material where young trees are thinned out or older ones felled, there does not seem much chance of survival'. By the beginning of the Second World War only nine wood-turners survived in the Chilterns to keep this rural craft alive.

A glimpse of their life emerges from another memory of George Dean who recalls that 'it was a problem in the winter getting enough work prepared outside by daylight for the evening lighting up as we called it.' 'The jays would always shriek a warning of strangers approaching.' 'Those thatched workshops were quite picturesque during the various seasons, the white shavings on the walls and the yellowish thatch showing up amid the sombre beech trees. Once a flock of pigeons descended on the trees around our shops just after dark. The noise of their flapping wings was alarming as they settled in the tree-tops, too exhausted to heed us very much as we worked by candlelight in our primitive way.'

Chapter Three

FROM COTTAGE INDUSTRY TO FACTORY

The chair industry was among the earliest to use a form of mass-production to speed up its work, and the Windsor chair is a good example of this. Many different people made the individual parts before the chair was assembled. In earlier days the parts were sent to London to be made up, then later to the new Wycombe factories. Later still the parts went to Wales and the Midlands, and at one time there was even a great business in sending chairs to Australia and other parts of the Empire in sections, all ready to be glued together on arrival.

Among the Chilterns, these legs, made so laboriously by the bodgers, were brought down to the factory to be joined up with the parts made by other artisans. The solid wooden chair seats made by the 'bottomer', were cut into shape from the elm planks cut in the saw pits, the planks being held rigid with iron holdfasts on a solid bench. The tool used to cut the shape was the frame-saw, an all round popular saw with a blade which was set in the centre of the square frame, or at the side. This saw blade could be removed and threaded through a hole in the wood when sawing intricate shapes or patterns. The names it gathered over the years were legion, including the accepted Up-and-down-saw, 'Dancing Betty' and the more unusual 'Jesus Christ Saw' which takes this name from the fact that when using it 'you did keep on a-bowing to Him'. One of these saws, now in the High Wycombe Museum, has been worn away at the place at which it was held, almost to breaking point. The saw was made originally by a lad of twelve and it was used by him as 'man and boy' until he retired at the age of seventy two!

The chair seat was now placed on the floor and using an adze, the 'bottomer' hacked into the heart of the seat, cutting against the grain with rhythm and precision to remove the excess wood and create the comfortable saddle shape for which the Windsor chair is noted. The adze was a type of axe with a cutting edge which was curved and dished, and using this tool the original two inch thick plank which forms the seat was in parts reduced to only three-quarters to half an inch. To do this, the tool has to be exceptionally sharp, and the workman must be extra careful, for there is always a chance that he might end up like Billy 'No-Toes' Neville,

The bottomer cut away the spare wood from the seat using a curved adze.

The wheelsplat has been cut and the workman cleans and finishes off the design with a file.

a local bottomer and a Primitive Methodist Lay Preacher. He lost his toes when adzing seats, so when Thomas Glenister introduced his first machine-adzer, it was christened Billy Neville and Mr. Glenister remarked that this machine wouldn't cut off anybody's toes!

The bow, which is the eye-catching feature of the bow-back chair is often made of yew. A suitable length was boiled in a tank to make it supple and then bent around a shaping block and pegged into position until dry. Some more adept workers did not need to use the block, but could bend the bow and simply tie the two ends together with a piece of cord. At times when a hard wood bow was used, such as with a mahogany chair, it might be necessary to make the curve in two or even three stages, allowing the bow to dry between each attempt.

With the use of spokeshaves the bow would be cleaned into shape ready for its job of supporting the back stick and the decorated splat. One of the chief differences between the American and English Windsor chair is the presence of this ornamental splat or banister in the English style. Its pattern, which might include the familiar wheel, the Prince of Wales

Bending a grown yew stake for a windsor bow. The stake, with others, has been previously boiled to render it supple.

feather or an elaborate Gothic pattern, is always an important feature of the chair. The splats were made using a paper or wooden pattern, the workman often cutting three or four at a time with a bow saw. For every part of the design, a fresh hole must be bored and the bow saw blade inserted to cut the required pattern. Some of the more elaborate splats required twelve to fifteen separate holes and saw cuts before they were finished. Wooden patterns in the High Wycombe Museum carry such pencilled messages as 'Please supply 24 Banisters to pattern, Thursday if Possible *most urgent*' so the rush and hustle of the workshop had its crisis times then just as now.

By this time the 'framer' or 'benchman' was completing the legging up, which was the job of assembling the seats, legs and stretcher into the underseat. He drilled the holes for the joints with the spoon drills which hang over the bench. This spoon-bit was a favourite with the framer as it does not split the wood and it can be started at almost any angle. As considerable pressure is required to make the hole, a breast bib made of hardwood and shaped to take the head of the brace was worn with a leather harness across the chest. If such a support wasn't used, it was

The wooden breast-bib is used to protect the chest.

possible for the pressure to rupture surface blood vessels and precipitate bleeding and considerable discomfort for the worker.

Before the modern brace was developed which takes a variety of bits, a separate brace was made for each size. These could number ten to fifteen in all, and the bits were sharpened with file. As the continual sharpening altered, in time, the size of the bits, they became known by the job they did, rather than by a given size. For example the bit used to cut the holes to take the stretcher would be called the stretcher bit, and another might be the legging bit.

Using a number of spokeshaves the seat was further smoothed, first came the curved blade of the 'travisher', then the 'cleaning off' iron. This was followed by a scraper with a vertical blade named a 'devil'. Finally using a scraper and sandpaper a satin finish was achieved.

The spoon drills again come into use as the benchman bored the holes to receive the stocks, bows and arms. These parts have their ends oven dried in order that they will shrink no further. When they are socketed into the holes in the seat and in the bow the holes will tighten their hold around the joints as they dry out and so strengthen the chair.

After the seat has been shaped and the holes for the legs bored, the whole underseat is 'legged-up' with a framers hammer.

As a chairmaker became more proficient he soon realised that given initiative and a few basic tools he too could start up in business and so a number of sheds in back gardens saw the birth of prosperous businesses. But to commence a full scale chairmaking concern more than this was needed. A workshop was required, usually with a brick built ground floor with a wooden first floor overhead. Also needed was a store to keep timber, a stable for a horse and a cart from which to sell the chairs which were to be made. With all these he was in business.

Frequently the success of such a firm depended entirely upon the ability to sell the chairs quickly and return to the workshop with the money in time to pay the wages for his men. When the Saturday deadline could not be met, then 'Master's sure to pay on Monday' was the poor wife's excuse when begging for more on credit at the grocer's shop for weekend food.

The horse and cart played a large part in the progress of the trade, and the men found themselves having to load and unload the waggons in turn. 'When a load of timber was brought into the yard, the men used to have to set down tools and get the timber in and they weren't paid for that either; we used to be the same with the loading of a load of chairs up, they used to have to send so many out, so many in a gang; well, all wasted time! and if there was a lot of turned stuff from the country, you would have to go out and do your share. They used to occupy sometimes one of these loads of chairs, about six layers all done up in straw'.

The personal view of another worker was 'as to unloading, well, you wanted to work indoors and that chair stuff wouldn't get up and walk in to you, and when your chairs were made, they were precious little use to the master or you till they were up on the van and away'. Still, there was always the possibility that if it was a large load, an order for a pint of beer all round would come from the master, when the grumbling would be muffled.

A regular carrier with his horse-drawn cart was Harry Longford of Northend, Bucks, who was delivering chair parts from 1922 to 1958. As he was also a general carrier he would often do shopping for the villagers, delivering parcels and sometimes carry passengers as well. On Monday and Thursday evenings he would collect the sacks of chair parts from the bodgers in the Turville Woods for delivery in Wycombe on the Tuesdays and Fridays. The weather could make a usually pleasant trip quite hazardous in the winter months. With ice and snow around, Harry Longford and his wife who sometimes accompanied him, might be forced to walk by the waggon for most of the eight miles into Wycombe, with Mrs. Longford ready on the steeper hills to slip the chock behind the rear wheel when the horse rested. Harry Longford could also recall an earlier carrier, a David Bristol of Northend, who in the mid-nineteenth century, is said to have hauled timbers from the woods with a team of donkeys!

The past lingers on in the nineteenth century wooden factories which abound in the Chilterns. They still function well, often converted to modern woodworking methods, or diverted to entirely different industrial processes. These rural factories were a far cry from the picture of the London workshop of Mr. Seddons which was drawn by Sophie von la

The typical small chairmaker's workshop, littered with tools, chair parts, splats, bows and partly completed chairs.

Roche in 1786. Here the owner 'employs four hundred apprentices on any work connected with the making of household furniture – joiners, carvers, mirror-workers, upholsterers, girdlers who moulded the bronze into graceful patterns and locksmiths. All these are housed in a building with six wings. Seddons, foster-father to four hundred employees seemed a man who has become intimate with the quality of woods, has appreciated the value of all his own people's labour and toil, and is forever creating new forms.'

The workshops in the country districts had few frills when they were built, no heat except for the slow combustion stove which kept the polishing shop just warm enough to ensure the work kept moving. The buildings were rather primitive, low-pitched and very narrow, with the staircase outside to the upper floor to save space inside. No glass in the windows, just panels of oiled calico which enabled a gentle light to enter, but did not invite the workmen to waste time gawping out on the yard or street.

The introduction of steam in the 1860's was the means of helping in the removal of the main bottleneck in the furniture industry, the conversion of the timber into planks, for which the circular saw came into use. It was only possible to use it on butts of about two foot six inches, and the pits were still used to cut the larger trunks in half before bringing them in for the circular saw to take over. But in time the band saw was introduced, followed by the jig saw which by the use of several blades, could cut a trunk into many planks in one action. Bert Mullet, writing after sixty years in the trade when he retired in 1971, mentions the use of the hand-operated band saw which required three people to turn it besides the man actually sawing out the wood who used a treadle connected to the drive. He was sometimes on this job for an hour or more and by that time he felt like collapsing.

As the supply of prepared timbers was speeded up, it allowed more men to be employed and so for a while very few other innovations were introduced. The use of machinery added a battery of overhead belts, driving shafts and pulleys to the many hazards already present in the workshop. This, with the unguarded machines, the highly volatile and inflammable polishes and paints and the sawdust underfoot, would have been a factory inspector's nightmare. One important machine came with the introduction of the seat borer, which would bore the 60-70 holes necessary for the seat caner in a matter of seconds instead of the former laborious hand boring process. Indeed one boring machine in use in 1890 was estimated to be capable of boring 35,000 holes a day!

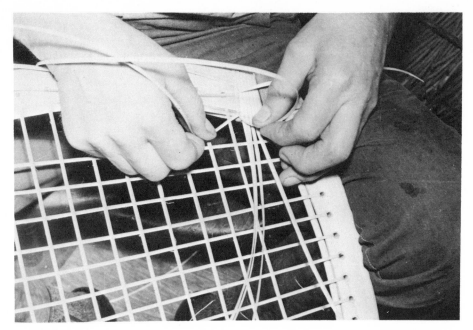

A seat being caned with willow skein; the doubling is done and the setting just being completed.

The use of cane for seating, which had been popular in Stuart times, saw a rapid revival in the second quarter of the nineteenth century. The mechanisation of the lace industry took much business from the cottage workers, and the women were quick in transferring their interest to chair caning. The preparation of the canes which was often done by the men, involved the removal of the knots in the cane and the splitting and removal of the pith or wisp. the split cane was then passed under horizontal razor-sharp blades to produce the clean cut even strip necessary to weave the pattern.

The task of caning could be done by women and children, and boys and girls as young as seven years of age would help at home in this task. In better class work, more intricate patterns would be specified, but the basic tools and methods would be the same. The caner sat on a very low stool, then drawing the chair seat she was about to cane up to her knees, she held it in place. This enabled her to move the chair seat around, yet still remain in a reasonably restful position.

The first operation was the 'doubling', or the initial knotting of the ends and the passing of the cane in a continuous double line through the holes in the back rail to the front rail. The 'setting' was the weaving of more cane across from the holes in the side pieces, creating the basic pattern of squares. The next move is the 'crossing' when the cane is interwoven diagonally each way to strengthen the seat and make it flexible. Now comes the 'pegging' when every other hole around the seat is pegged with a small deal peg to keep the cane firm. Finally the 'beading' which is a wide strip of cane is used to 'edge the job off' and cover up the holes and generally tidy up the pattern.

Before the First World War it was a common sight to see women sitting at their front door caning chairs, which, when completed, would be carried back to the factory in bundles of six. They were stacked in such a way that a number could be moved by slipping an arm through the lowest chair and lifting them wholesale. Very few firms employed caners at the factories before 1900, as most of the caning could be done at home. The price paid around that time was one and a half pence per chair.

The splitting of cane was also 'put out' to be completed at home, round cane was collected from an agent, in Wycombe from the Van Inn in Oxford Street, and returned when 'made off' in the required size. No money changed hands, but the proprietor credited the workers to the amount and supplied groceries or other necessities against the work done.

Another form of seating was rush matting, the familiar material of the common church seat. This work was a very dirty job in comparison with caning. The rushes came from the marshes fringing the rivers on the Oxfordshire border, where they would be harvested and dried when they had reached a height of six to eight feet. Vans then carried them to the chairmaking centres. The rush seat makers worked amongst the dust and mud, for the rushes were dampened in order to make them workable, in an atmosphere which was far from healthy, twisting and stuffing and joining the rushes into a comfortable if not beautiful seat. The rushes also gave off an unpleasant odour which gave rise to the comment that 'you could smell a matter a mile off'.

Other variations in material include the use of finer rushes from Holland, willow seating and straw matting. With the straw matting the rushes were covered with split lengths of straw which might be a natural colour or dyed in order to weave an attractive pattern. Occasionally very fine work was demanded and one miniature chair had to be delicately seated in in silk, a task which took much patience and time before it was completed. The cottage craft nature of caning still exists today, and in recent years dining chairs are losing their upholstered seats and being caned instead, while as recently as the 1930's children picked up seat frames and cane at the factory on their way home from school for their parents to work on overnight, ready to be returned completed next morning.

While the presence of the Buckinghamshire beech highlights the reason for the provincial chair industry being centred in the Chilterns, the date and circumstances relating to the arrival of chairmakers in that area is not clear. It is certain that they were practising their craft in the Chiltern towns in the early 1700's, for in the Parish Accounts of West Wycombe against the date of December 17th 1732 is the payment of 6s 6d to David Pisis (Pusey) for a 'wins chair ordered by Vestry'. This reference to a Windsor chair located in the ledgers of the Overseers of the Poor by Herbert Green, predates by many years other references for that area, and is a very early identification of the Windsor type.

In the late eighteenth century the Chipping Wycombe Parish documents record: —

Parish Accounts 1793 . . . paid a chair maker that was ill   5.0
Mary Phillips for nursing the chairmakers wife   7.6
For the chairmaker   15.0

So at this date the chairmakers were active, even if this particular one was on the Parish 'dole' queue! The Chairmaster was also present in the records, for in 1790 the same accounts note a payment to: —

Mr. Samuel Treacher — half a part of the wood used in
the hall   10.6

This Samuel Treacher, who was born in 1769 is linked with Thomas Widgington in establishing the first chair factory in the area. The date of this undertaking is in doubt, but it is most probably earlier than that of 1805 which is recorded in a stained glass window in the High Wycombe Town Hall. In the year 1798 a list of men aged fifteen to sixty was compiled by the High Sheriff of Bucks, which recorded thirty-three men listed as chairmakers. If the figures for the Borough of High Wycombe are added to the Parish and to West Wycombe, over fifty chairmakers appear to have been working in the district. As the Treacher family were given as chairmakers in the 1784 British Directory, the presence of the craft must date back to the 1750's in some form or the other.

Of course the chief centre of furniture both rural and fine was London, and it is probable that the Chiltern industry has grown with an influx of craftsmen from the City. In later years there was an exodus to the provinces, and between the years 1801-1960 J. L. Oliver records that High Wycombe produced more chairs than all the London manufacturers put together. It should not be forgotten that these London chairmakers also made rural chairs, and in a hamlet such as Hammersmith in 1813 'a very great number of those wooden chair known by the designation of Windsor chairs are made here, together with rustic seats, &c by Webb and Bruce and Mr. Carter'.

The particular significance to the furniture industry of the rural chair was its development as a wood-turner's chair rather than a joiner's chair, a factor which was important in separating the chairmaker from other woodworking trades. From the early years of the 1790's until 1877 the number of factories mainly producing chairs in High Wycombe grew to almost a hundred which, according to one authority, turned out over 4,700 chairs per day. As the improvement of road surfaces and the coming of railways eased travel to other parts of the country, so the market expanded and the industry flourished.

Some of the orders were quite remarkable. When the great American evangelists Moody and Sankey toured Britain in 1873-5 a rush order for 19,200 chairs for their revival meeting was accepted and finished in a few weeks. These had to be sent to London by van, as it was felt that they would take too long if dispatched by rail. Another order was placed for 8,000 chairs for Crystal Palace, while in 1874 Walter Skull made 4,000 rush seated chairs at a cost of four shillings each for St. Paul's Cathedral, and a further 6,000 chairs for military purposes.

These government contracts were important to the town, and during the First World War orders for wooden rifles for recruit training, ammunition boxes, propellors, and other components for the newly introduced aircraft kept the craftsmen working.

Strangely enough, one of the foremost helpers in improvement and mechanisation was fire! The wooden buildings with their numerous oil lamps, combustion stoves, loose shavings, polishes, cane and rush cuttings, created great hazards for fire so that conflagrations frequently took place. This was not always to the Chairmaster's disadvantage, as it enabled him, if fully insured, to invest in new buildings and tools. Sometimes tragedy took place; in January 1922 Gomme's premises in High Wycombe were gutted by fire, destroying much of their new machinery and doing damage to the value of £30,000.

The workmen themselves frequently had losses, and in a fire at Cox and Barretts the workers lost all their tools and equipment. A fund was established to help them, and this raised sufficient money to buy new tools for the men and also give a shilling to each of the caning children thrown out of work by the fire.

Such a hazard was always present, and one can feel great sympathy with Benjamin North of West Wycombe. When on business in the Midlands he arrived back to his lodgings one day to find a telegram waiting for him which read 'Shops all on fire; come home as soon as possible'. In his autobiography he adds wryly 'The damage was about £4,000 and I was insured for £1,500 only'.

Chapter Four .

THE APPRENTICES AND THE CUSTOMS OF THE TRADE

'My parents should give him twenty pounds premium, and I should receive no wages the first year, but five shillings per week for the second year'. Thus runs the account of a Midlands apprenticeship agreement of the early 1830's. A similar indenture for Wycombe of 1824 is also very specific in laying down rules to be followed by the apprentice during his period of service:—

> He shall not commit fornication nor contract matrimony within the said term, he shall not play cards or dice tables or any other unlawful games wherebye his masters may have loss with his goods or otherwise, he shall neither buy nor sell, he shall not haunt taverns nor playhouses.

In return the master promises to 'find, provide and allow the said apprentice, competent and sufficient meat, drink, apparel, lodging, washing and other things necessary and fit for an apprentice'. It was also agreed that the master should 'teach and instruct or cause to be taught or instructed in the art of Windsor chair framing' or whatever part of the trade to which the boy was contracted. The wages for the apprentice in 1824 were very low, and almost fifty years later they were basically the same, which is a rather sobering thought.

Quite often the Parish Vestry of a village might try to get orphan children off their hands by paying the apprentice premium themselves. This was done when the Trustees of the Lady Jane Boys Charity placed a poor boy from Great Missenden as apprentice to Thomas Widgington of Chipping Wycombe in 1809. As a master would require a fairly heavy premium, children of poorer parents could not always be apprenticed, so they were forced to take such menial jobs as were available in the trade. Tom Sutton recalls starting work in a small firm at the age of nine years and two months, and earning a wage of one shilling and sixpence a week. When the Education Act of 1870 was passed, he was supposed to go to school half time, but living as he did in a small village, this was conveniently overlooked.

The problem of declining apprenticeships was highlighted by William Parnell in 1888. 'There is scarcely a legally bound apprentice in London

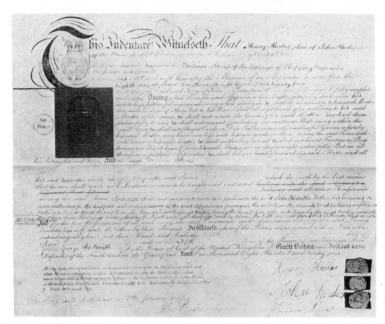

The Indenture of Henry Heales who was apprenticed to William Steers in 1824 to be taught the art of a carpenter and joiner.

now at the present moment. Boys go in the shops as errand boys, to sweep up the shavings and run errands for the men, and in a little while as they get bigger and stronger they get a jack plane put into their hands, and they assist that man on any particular job he may be working on'.

The children who went to school usually ended up in the trade. John Mayes notes that out of the fifty-two children who left the Wycombe British School in 1854, twenty-two went into the chair factories. Some started as errand boys, others in the polishing shops and some in the carving shops. One carver complained bitterly of the time spent teaching the youngsters coming into the trade. 'I never had a halfpenny out of the boys, the Boss had all the profits'.

The hours of work were long, well over sixty hours a week. One Chairmaster recalls they were 'at our benches at six o'clock and did not leave off work till eight o'clock p.m. including Saturday', while another remembered work 'started anything from 5.30 to 6.0 a.m., breakfast being taken 7.30 to 8.0 a.m. Then at 10.0 a.m., those who were not teetotallers, and they were very few, took ten minutes for beer and bread and cheese, often accompanied by a good strong onion. From 12.0 to 1.0 p.m. we had

The workmen, chairframers and seven young boys, standing outside a chair factory c.1870 showing four of the chair designs made at the factory.

dinner and from 3.30 to 4.0 p.m. tea. After that work would go on until 7.0 p.m.'. He adds that the hours were not so rigid as now, for they . worked on piece work and there was no clocking in and out.

But although men in some shops came and went as they wished, others established their own self-discipline. Mr. Barnes of Stokenchurch would expect to adze two dozen seats before breakfast in the summer when work started at 6.30 a.m. and one dozen in the winter when he started at 7.30 a.m. There was also little time to stand still for the chair framer who would be given the parts for a dozen lath-back chairs. He would make the tenons for all the parts, cut the joints, fit the stretchers, leg-up the chairs, fit the laths, stands and comb. For this work, which should be completed in ten to eleven hours, he would receive a payment of five shillings.

As holidays were not paid for, they were seldom welcome, as any time off meant saving up on an already stretched budget. As late as 1938 this was still a grievance. 'We have not any factory in Wycombe which has a recognised holiday, anytime of the year' reports E. Rolph in the NAFTA News. 'Very often one can hear men and women . . . say things unprintable about the 'glorified lockout' at August week. Not 10% of furniture workers go on holidays — they cannot afford to do so. We urge

The workbenches of the chairmakers were covered with tools, the spokeshaves can be seen on the wall, whilst the spoondrills, saws and chisels hang in front of the windows.

all workers to join their respective Trade Unions to bring about payment for all holidays'.

Wages by the turn of the twentieth century were about four shillings a week. Of course there was considerable moving from firm to firm. If there was a good workman at one workshop, another master on hearing of his ability might offer him another half-penny or a penny an hour in order to entice him to his factory.

Children, as well as starting work at an early age, often did work after school in order to earn money and learn the trade. A child could earn a new penny per week for chair packing. One lad started working from 4.30 to 7.30 p.m. and recalls sometimes staying on after 7.30 in the evening to make wooden wedges. These were split with the grain and dried on the stove and he was able to make a gross an hour, for the princely rate of one penny a gross. The youngsters were encouraged by the men and Mr. Barnes while still at school was taught to use the pole-lathe and could turn a Windsor leg before he was old enough to start work. He also came back after 6.30 in the evening and recalls making up chairs at a rate of one shilling a dozen chairs. Thomas Parker, who started work in London in

1894 earned a wage of one shilling a week. His dinner at the corner cookshop of beef and potatoes cost him seven pence a week with an extra halfpenny for bread.

There were many special customs associated with Victorian factory life. A particular annoyance was the demand for light money. The windows of many of the workshops were not glazed, but covered with calico or light hessian which necessitated artificial light quite early in the winter evenings. The charge for oil for the lamps was sometimes eightpence a week for each man, and when one boss introduced gas lighting, a charge of sixpence a week was still extorted.

A further payment which in this day and age seems rather strange was the charge for benchroom. Each workman who required to work at a bench surface was required to pay two shillings a week. A similar custom at Nottingham expected a new man to pay his 'footing', which was a sum of two shillings which he had to produce before his fellow workers would allow him to commence any job. In one instance a man had his chest of tools taken out of the workshop and hidden at the end of the saw pit until this payment was made. The demand for money did not stop there, for in some shops the new lad might find that 'having cut the wood for the table, I was told that I must pay a shilling for them to drink my health and also that they expected my father to pay a sovereign towards a binding supper . . . In fact every fresh job that I had not made one like it before, I had to pay a shilling or I should not be allowed to make it'.

Each man had to supply his own tools, but also had to pay two pence a week for the use of the grindstone. Another halfpenny was levied to pay for the services of the errand boy who fetched and carried and made some attempts to keep things clean and the shop hygienic. One of the worst jobs a young lad could do was the burning-in or the staining of the parts of a Windsor chair before it was assembled. Each piece was dipped in a tank which contained a solution of nitric acid which produced the rich Venetian red finish which was so popular. One chairmaker who did this task got the acid in his fingernails and on his fingers 'and I laid abed and cried more than one night with the pain'.

In such conditions trouble inevitably broke out amongst the men from time to time, and if this came to a head the practice in the Nottingham shops was to call together a court by striking a holdfast with a hammer. 'Upon hearing the sound, all the men from the various rooms would come together into the room where the sound came from to try the case by a jury consisting of all the men on the premises'. One man was chosen as judge by a show of hands, and which ever side was found to be at fault had to pay a fine of not less than one shilling. But if it had been a very hot day and the men were thirsty, it was not unusual for a fine of four or five shillings to be announced to be spent on drink before justice was achieved!

In cases where a man was unusually disagreeable, the rest of the men might well send him to Coventry. They never reckoned to take anyone back from Coventry for less than five shillings, and sometimes even as much as ten shillings.

In order to get the best out of the craftsmen, the owner of the factory sometimes farmed out certain processes. At one workshop the Foreman Polisher was paid a set amount to get a certain amount of work done. He would pay the polishers out of his own pocket, and if there was any surplus, he would keep it. He would take men on and give them so much an hour, and the master had nothing to do with the fixing of their wages.

In the country districts where the chairs had to be transported long distances to the markets, horse-drawn carts and vans were used, while in the London workshops the chairmakers often did this transporting themselves. Before Frederick Parker moved to Wycombe he used to hire flat-topped handcarts at two pence an hour to deliver furniture within the Metropolis, and it was Harry Parker's job to supervise the loading. He would often accompany the two workmen pushing it for miles through the London streets to its destination. At times, when the truck was not available and a delivery was urgent, the poor workman was loaded like a donkey with a large box ottoman all of six foot in length on his back and made to stagger with it from Curtain Road to Maples.

In Wycombe the waggon train of chair-loaded vans would plod in a very surefooted way out of Wycombe at eight to nine o'clock in the evening on a return trip to London which would take up to thirty-six hours in all. The drivers would start in earnest after a last drink at the 'King of Prussia' and there might be thirty or forty waggons lined up ready to start out for London, thirty miles away.

The first stop would be at the 'French Horn' at Gerrards Cross. Here the horses would be baited or fed, and rest for an hour and a half to two hours before starting out again for 'The White Hart', Southall, where they would bed down until five o'clock in the morning. Now the train of vehicles would slowly move along the road to Shepherd's Bush where breakfast would be eaten, from there on the vans travelled and delivered chairs to Maples and other shops until the last chair was unloaded, which could be as far as Ilford and Romford, in Essex, east of London.

The horses had made the journey so often that only the driver of the

When the chair waggons left Wycombe they were loaded high with the chairs wrapped in straw five or six layers high.

first van needed to stay awake, the rest sleeping amid the furniture and straw while their horses followed patiently through the night. Sometimes these trips might be more eventful. Montague Blamey took one load to London from Wycombe during the 1913 'Lock-out' and when he started out things were so touch and go that he had an escort of six mounted police, six foot police, a Superintendent and a Sergeant. They accompanied the van to Gerrards Cross, and then it was escorted by different police forces until all the chairs were unloaded at Stratford, in East London.

The wintry weather often caused discomfort. On one return trip it was snowing heavily and when his horse fell near Acton, the driver had to walk the horse very carefully all the way from there to Gerrards Cross in order to keep it upright. As the 'French Horn' hove into sight he was 'so thunderingly dog-tired I said to him 'Blow you, if you fall down, you fall down' and so let him pick his way to the stables by himself!'

Few of the customs of the trade seemed to favour the workman, but one which did was the practice of allowing a workman about to be married to make his own 'marriage' chair. It was made with timbers

Joe More's lath-back chair made on the occasion of his marriage c.1890 from fruit woods.

The tokens of James Gomme dated 1811 and of W. Skull & Co., Grocers & Tea Dealers of Wycombe.

chosen with care for which only a nominal charge was made, and such a chair, made of fruitwood and elm can be seen in the High Wycombe Museum. However, when this custom was mentioned to a group of retired chairmakers, they were most scornful, adding that in their early days the 'Gaffer never gave 'owt away'.

One of the chief causes for complaint was the late payment of wages. The early chairmakers were often publicans, having their workshops in the Inn yard. Consequently the payment of wages took place in the public house. If the master delayed paying, the men would be left hanging around, and not wishing to stand there empty-handed, would not be backward in having a few more drinks marked up on the slate against their future wages. Reports in local papers over the years reflect the anger which existed surrounding this problem. One wife complained of the bad example set by her husband to their twelve-year-old son, when both of them come home tottering, having drunk a good part of both their wages.

The master might also run a grocers shop on the side, and payment of part of the week's wages could well be in the form of tokens to be drawn on this shop. They were called Tommy shops, and the purpose of the Trucks Acts was to eliminate this kind of racket, but it took a long time a-dying. The 'chitty' or tokens could be converted into cash, but at a lower amount than the face value, so that an eight shilling token might only fetch five shillings, which effectively reduced the value of the take-home pay even further. Another problem to be dealt with was the scarcity of copper change in coins of the realm. To overcome this shopkeepers issued a very wide variety of tokens which could be used as small change. As these were of a very local nature, bearing the name of the dealer and the town of origin, they were often only redeemable in full at the shop from which they were issued, and the workman paid in such tokens might easily find himself at a disadvantage, finding that he could only change them or buy goods at something less than their face value. Two nineteenth century tokens were issued from High Wycombe of this nature, the first has the legend 'James Gomme MDCCCXI' on one side with a picture of Wycombe Guildhall, and on the reverse 'High Wycombe and Buckinghamshire Token XII pence' and the image of a swan. The other is much more simple, the obverse carries a portrait of the Queen Victoria and the legend 'Victoria Queen of Great Britain' and the reverse the words 'W. Skull & Co. Grocers & Tea Dealers, High Wycombe'.

An attempt to change the payday to Thursday was made in Wycombe in 1860, when in a letter in the local newspaper Mr. James Hussey argued that it would be better for shopping at the weekend. He added that the present Saturday payment system 'brings such a number of people into the town that those who idle instead of work, flock in at the same time to entrap the unwary and lure the youth'.

It seems unlikely that the workmen needed any tuition in such matters, for the absenteeism on Mondays in Wycombe was so notorious that the day became nicknamed St. Monday. Few except the poor apprentices worked after dinner on Monday. The majority of the men formed gangs and visited the local pubs, playing games or contests in which a pint of beer might be the prize. In the more popular pubs the frying pan was put on the stove about 4.0 p.m. and a great fry-up of bacon, eggs and liver was produced at a cost of sixpence a portion. One polisher recalls that any man with a shilling in his pocket on a Monday wouldn't be seen dead at work. Another chairframer told how he used to work with a man that got drunk every Saturday and Sunday, and when he came in on Monday he said 'Ah Bill! never no more, never no more, lend me two shillings' and off he would go again. From Tuesday to Saturday evening he would work like a Trojan, then on Monday again it was 'Ah never no more!'.

The growth of the factory system brought its moral problems. In 1857 the Vicar of High Wycombe called a meeting in the Guildhall 'To consider what measures could be adopted to correct a growing source of depravity from the constant association of young persons of both sexes in our manufactories'. The conclusions drawn up at the meeting included the setting up of separate shops for male and female workers, and a half an hour difference between the finishing times for both sexes.

The Unions came on to the scene in the early Victorian period and the atmosphere of the time is wrapped up in an anonymous song of the 1870's:—

> 'Says the master to me Is it true, I am told
> Your name on the books of the Union's enrolled.
> I can never allow that a workman of mine
> With wicked destroyers of peace should combine
> I now give you warning, in what you're about,
> I shall put my foot down and stamp it all out.
> So you must take notice, for sure you can see
> And decide now at once for the Union, or me.'

The Chairmakers Protection Society was formed in Wycombe in 1855, the impressive certificate of membership carried the motto (in Latin) 'We stand for the right to work'. From early days the men kept watch on these rights. 'They told me I must on no account do a job quicker than they had been in the habit of doing, they could dull your tools! I had to veneer the rim of a job in which I excel'd, having done many before. However on this the glue would not stick as it had evidently in my absence been rubbed over with grease'. Times clearly haven't changed.

The Chairmakers Protection Society had a Mechanics Loan Society which enabled workmen to raise money for the purchase of tool kits, and in Wycombe in 1861 it went so far as to form a workers' co-operative which claimed a capital of £5,000 in £1 shares. But the chief difficulty the Unions met in representing the chairmaking trade arose from the wide variety of jobs contained within it. When negotiations to standardise the wage structure were being discussed in 1872, the printed list of prices suggested for consideration covered two hundred and fifty separate processes.

When some of the Chairmasters agreed to the prices, a group of men formed a procession 'headed by a band and with flags flying, to the Rye, and on the way, as they passed the shops of the Masters who had already

The membership card of the High Wycombe Chairmakers' Protection Society, founded in 1855.

The pickets on duty outside Holland and Johnson's in Wycombe during the dispute which lasted from October 1913 to March 1914.

paid the prices asked, the men cheered themselves hoarse, but the remaining factories were passed in silence, the band also ceasing to play'. The attitude of the bosses is apparent in the comment of one Chairmaster 'if a man had a farthing an hour rise he would dance, if he had a halfpenny he would jump with joy'. However, during the history of the chair industry in Wycombe, a number of strikes and the protracted lock-out of 1913 give a different view of industrial peace.

Some firms managed to avoid trouble. W. B. Haines was proud to recall that 'the only time this firm has stopped work was when we were stopped by the electricity supply in the winter of 1947, and there's never been a minute lost on this firm, and we've been here 63 years'. In order to retain staff during the slump periods, they stock-piled chairs and in 1932 and 1933 the firm had as many as 2,000 chairs in their storerooms.

Five years later the situation was better, but even so the union official in Wycombe, C. F. Hawkins, had worries 'I have always been anxious to get as much work as possible and have even jeopardised my prospects in the next world to protect the district . . . all districts are hungry for work now and the more alert disqualify each other'.

The girls working in the cane and rush seating shops had an equally hard time. Starting work at the age of twelve, it would sometimes be three years before they finished learning their trade and could earn good money on 'good best' cane work. The piece work rate for caning was twopence three-farthings a seat in 1900, whilst a rush matter would get sixpence a chair. If very fine work was required the price would go up to one shilling or one shilling and threepence. Money varied, and one caner started at four shillings and sixpence a week, yet later managed to earn four to five pounds a week when doing best work.

Although the cane and rushes were provided, the deal pegs used in finishing off had to be supplied by the caning girls. They also used their own tools, and had their own low caning stool. One rush matter worked for many months on chair seats for the maiden voyage of the *'Titanic'* which sank so tragically in 1912 with a loss of 1,513 lives. Her first knowledge of the disaster came in a comment from the Master. 'I reckon the mermaids do sit on your chairs now, for the *Titanic* has gone down'.

These girls, now in their sixties and seventies, still remember with affection the jokes, fun and songs of the old days. And when they get together, the familiar 'Wycombe Caning Girls Song' is frequently brought out for an airing:—

"T'was in the middle of Mendy Street a charming girl I met,
She'd deep blue eyes and golden hair and her voice was
    soft and sweet.
She blushed at me, then looked away, and never did she mind,
For underneath her arm she had a small bundle of cane."

Refrain

"I nearly broke my heart, never wish to see her again,
That blue eyed girl with her hair in curl,
I met with a bundle of cane.
And then we did agree to meet again on Tom Birts Hill,
To talk of happy moments past and sweeter memories still.
And talk of happy days in store which made us sudden stop,
Would you condescend to marry a girl who works in a caning
    shop.
Now all young men take my advice, when to Wycombe Town you go
Don't talk to pretty caning girls or else they'll serve you so.
They'll steal away your heart, my boys, and well they will be
    true.
Then with those blooming polishers, they'll bolt away from you."

Chapter Five

SALESMANSHIP AND MINIATURE CHAIRS

Few people can fail to appreciate the beauty and craftsmanship of miniature furniture, which exists either as dolls house furniture, travellers' samples or apprentice pieces. Children's doll-type furniture has been made for many centuries, and when Queen Mary's Dolls House was opened in 1922, it included a miniature cannon dated c.1580. This was the work of Michael Mann, a prominent Nuremberg armourer, and is one of the oldest travellers' samples known today. Such masters of the furniture world as Thomas Chippendale and architects such as Robert Adam did not think it beneath themselves to create special designs to be made in miniature. Much of this furniture was made, as indeed the boys train-set is today, more for the pleasure of parent than the child. I suspect that many of the dainty chairs and chests, which stand only inches high, graced the glass cabinets of the drawing room rather than the rooms of the well worn dolls' house in the nursery.

The diminutive Windsor chairs the Queen's Dolls House contains were made by craftsmen at Nicholls & Janes in 1920 at a time when an interest in making miniature furniture was very great. R. A. Janes commented that 'some of my most interesting work was done for Sir Edwin Lutyens, my albums are full of photographs of most unusual and beautiful things of his design what we had the pleasure of making, including many pieces that were made for Queen Mary's Dolls House'. The bow-back Windsor side chairs can be seen in the scullery, the linen room and the kitchen, while they are joined by bow-back arm chairs in the day nursery. Visitors to Windsor Castle can see these chairs in their Royal setting, while in High Wycombe Museum are displayed pattern chairs made at the same time, and miniature chairs from nine inches down to three-quarters of an inch in height.

Ten years after the opening of the Dolls House, the Wycombe Furniture Manufacturers Federation mounted an exhibition of miniature furniture with considerable success. Apparently during the depression of the 1930's, at a time when most factories were concerned with price rather than quality, letters in the local Wycombe press asked whether there were any craftsmen left, and what were they doing. This prompted the exhibition

A set of miniature Windsor chairs which were made by Nicholls and Janes in 1920 for the Queen Mary's Dolls' House at Windsor Castle. This duplicate set was made at the same time. The chairs are 3" high. *(High Wycombe Museum)*.

where a number of models proved that 'in spite of the machine age, their hands have not lost their cunning and that the individual workman in High Wycombe is still as great a craftsman as ever. Amazement has been expressed that model furniture accurate in every detail could be made on so small a scale. The overall measurement of any piece had not to exceed six inches square, but many of the pieces are much smaller than that'.

Recently I had the pleasure of seeing something of the recent work of Albert C. Lowe, who was one of the exhibitors. Now retired, he has been able to concentrate his craftsmanship upon a series of miniature chairs which illustrate the different chair styles to have appeared since Elizabethan times. They are seldom more than seven inches high and Albert Lowe has cut, carved, joined and upholstered with infinite care and considerable skill, chairs of Chippendale, Hepplewhite, Windsor and ladder-back designs, using such traditional woods as mahogany, beech, walnut and oak. It is often feared that these skills have been lost in an age of mass-production and machine tools, but these craftsmen can still turn a Windsor chair leg which is only an inch and a half long to a required pattern, cut and fit dovetail joints which are almost imperceptible in a manner truly worthy of the eighteenth century tradition.

It was this skill which was necessary when the joiner or cabinet-maker embarked upon his 'proof-piece' or apprentice-piece, which might be of great importance in his career. These examples of model furniture, which often took the form of cabinets, staircases or chests of drawers, if properly authenticated can prove most valuable, but alas, few truly come under this heading. Many pieces, if researched, would prove to be the work of amateur craftsmen and many others will often turn out to be travellers' samples or showpieces which were kept in the mid nineteenth century furniture shop for the use of customers.

The number of true apprentice-pieces which have survived is not large, originally it was a necessary culmination of the years of training received from a master-craftsman. In the rules of the Worshipful Company of Joiners of the City of London of 1572 it is stipulated that 'every apprentice was to serve two years as journeyman, and every man was to make his proof-piece'. As joiners didn't specialise in furniture-making until the seventeenth century, it is unlikely that any early pieces survived. By the end of the seventeenth century larger workshops existed in London, and the apprentice did not necessarily live in, being paid a wage, instead of receiving lodging and food. These were not apprentices in the fullest sense, and probably did not make these test pieces.

As furniture, especially the bigger pieces, was usually made to order, it would not be practical for the manufacturer to hold full-scale examples in his workshops of all his designs for the customers to select styles. Here the miniature show-piece became most useful, for if made to scale and in proper proportions, a shelf could hold quite a number, and indicate more clearly than hand-drawn catalogues the true shape, colour, texture and finish of a chest of drawers, bureau or tall-boy.

It was also not possible for the chair-salesman, setting out with his load of chairs, to hold sufficient styles on board for his customers to see for order purposes as he travelled the length and breadth of the country. Here again the miniature chair was used, for although by this time, catalogues were available, the customers of the 1870's were still anxious to see actual examples which showed the craftsmanship as well as the design of the chair they were about to purchase or order. These chairs were made to quarter-scale and stand about fifteen inches high, and examples have survived made as late as 1865. Unlike the smaller miniatures they are not so minute, and are not always as elegantly proportioned. The interest of these sample chairs was not appreciated by the descendants of some of the chairmakers who find them tucked away in their sheds or attics. Two examples which are on display at Wycombe represent the 'double C' balloon chair and a small folding chair with cane panels which were the only survivors salvaged from a garden bonfire after the family had decided upon a clearout of the rubbish they no longer wanted.

About the same time the hand-drawn and watercoloured pattern books were being shown to prospective buyers, with the printed catalogue,

Miniature mahogany smoker's bow library chair, made by A. C. Lowe, 6 inches high.

Miniature mahogany ladderback *(right)* 7¼ inches high and Chinese Chippendale mahogany armchair *(left)* 7 inches high, made by A. C. Lowe.

Travellers' sample of an upholstered chair based on the Restoration armchair. 12 inches high. *(High Wycombe Museum)*

Miniature Windsor bow-back armchair with heart shaped motif in the splat. Height 3½ inches. *(High Wycombe Museum)*

which was in use about 1850, becoming more widely used for sales. It is not often realised when using pictorial lists for identification purposes, that it was common practice to use a standard printed catalogue and simply overprint the manufacturers' name on the cover to make it appear to be his personal list. When asked for a chair which they may not have previously produced, a quick calculation would often have to be made to work out a price which could be met when they returned to the workshop. Sometimes in order to get a good sale chairs might be made almost at a loss. Mr. Haines recalls his father travelling down to Southampton and getting an order for 300-400 chairs at ten shillings and sixpence a bundle of six. When he told the purchaser it would be necessary to raise the price by 3d a dozen, the order was immediately torn up and thrown on the fire, and he got no more orders from that quarter.

The earliest catalogue in the High Wycombe Collection is dated 1849, and contains chairs designed and sold by Walter Skull of Wycombe. The illustrations are delicately drawn in pencil, often lined with ink and then coloured with watercolours. The designs of the beechwood chairs are beautifully tinted and the enamelled chairs are shown in black with gilded

Travellers' samples made 1865. *(left)* Double-C balloon chair 17 inches high *(right)* cane seated folding deck chair, size 14 inches high.

decoration picked out in gold and as bright now as when they were first shown to the customers.

Printed catalogues for 'fine' chairs such as Chippendale's 'Director' of 1762 and Shereton's 'Drawing Book' of the same date have been widely used by chair-makers, but with the exception of the designs given in Loudon's Encyclopedia of Cottage, Farmhouse, and Villa Furniture of 1833, few examples of early country chairs, middle-class and children's furniture have survived prior to the 1840's. In the catalogues available of Wycombe firms in the 1860's it is noticeable that over 300-400 styles are given. Few furniture manufacturers today could attempt to hold and re-make so many designs, and remain solvent. Some of the catalogues are in leaflet form, others, such as those of Glenisters and Benjamin North are quite large books with hard covers. In all cases only the design number is shown on the page, not even the name is quoted, and a printed insert giving the price and style would be handed out which could be easily altered when prices changed without altering the main catalogue.

Some of the catalogues appear in the form of broadsheets of up to three feet by two feet in size, and some smaller sheets contain only a

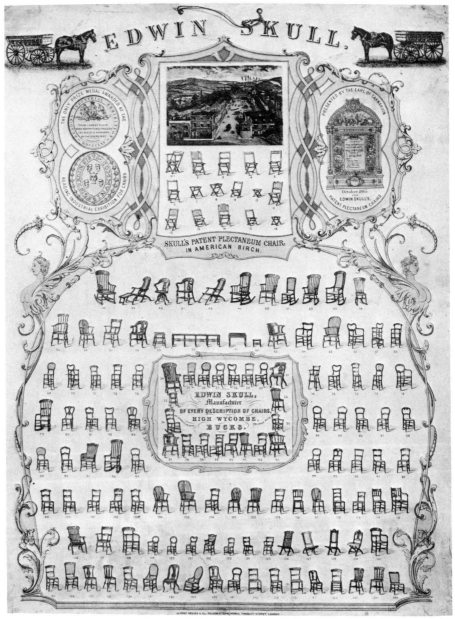

Edwin Skull's Broadsheet c.1863 which includes over 140 chairs. Note the waggons depicted at the top waiting to be loaded with chairs.

selection of the more popular designs. Some of the most interesting catalogues are the design and cost books which were used by the designers in making the estimates when planning new styles. A set of these books for the firm of Wm. Birch of High Wycombe relate to the period 1901-1905 giving designs and costs for the many chairs they produced during the Art Nouveau period. An elaborate broadsheet printed for Edwin Skull in c.1863 goes further than most and contains within its borders over one hundred and forty miniature drawings of the patterns available. Surmounting these designs is a tinted drawing of the horse-drawn waggons waiting to be loaded before leaving High Wycombe on their travels.

Seeing photographs of the unwieldy vehicles and bearing in mind the state of the roads a century ago, makes one wonder about the drivers who undertook this thankless task. One who recorded his memories was Benjamin North of West Wycombe, a former paper-maker who was thrown out of work by the introduction of machinery into that trade. He became a traveller in 1833 and his autobiography relates how he 'went to one Mr. Randel of Thame, who was a chair-turner, and gave him my service for a time at a shilling a day, so that I might learn another trade by which I could get an honest living'. Mr. Randel realised that North would at first be of little use in the workshop and 'knowing that I was painfully acquainted with the geography of my country' asked him to become his traveller. 'So I took my first journey with a load of chairs, starting from Thame in the night going through Wheatley, on to Headington, where I took my horse out and gave it the usual bait and also refreshed myself'. Carrying on he travelled through Witney, Burford to the 'beautiful town of Cheltenham' and so on to Tewkesbury. 'In Tewksbury I sold my chairs and returned home, thus finishing my first journey with satisfaction to my master'.

Being of a poetic turn of mind Benjamin could not resist turning his exploits into verse:

'Twas in the month of May,
From Wycombe we did start,
And Monday was the day,
When with our horse and cart,
We left our home to do our best
And with the Lord we left the rest.

First day was smooth and sweet,
Nothing did us annoy,
For the journey was a treat
As all was peace and joy
For all creation smiled around
And birds did sing with cheerful sound.

Next day was not so fair;
Now I will tell you why:
With me it did ill fare,
My horse did turn so shy;
By actions he did plainly say,
'I do not mean to go this way.'

His description of the trip, the towns through which he passed and his philosophical view towards the world in general took up a good few more verses until the poem concluded:—

In Leeds I sold my chairs,
And did more orders take,
Cleared out my timber wares,
And many friends did make.
My price was good, I now do tell,
Which satisfied my master well.

Not averse to making a little money on the side, Benjamin North also took with him other goods 'everybody knows that Royal Bucks is celebrated for lace-making, and people in my journey would ask me for it. I saw in this another way of turning an honest penny and opening a little branch of business'.

Most of the time he travelled alone, but occasionally he was in charge of two loads. This necessitated another driver as 'The regulations of the King's Highway required that one man should attend each team, and therefore someone had to go with me. My dear old friend Joseph Moorcock, who in the year 1837 suffered very much from rheumatic fever, now, being a little better. I thought it would do him good to go . . . we left the next morning for Leeds, and getting there safely put up at the Golden Cross. There we sold our chairs — all that we had left'. One day he was challenged by a well-known chair-maker when on his travels, 'Young man, your goods are not first class'. Benjamin quickly replied,

'No, but no doubt they are worth all I shall get for them'. He soon fell on his feet, and married a chair-maker's daughter, setting up in business himself in 1853.

Talking about the journeys made to sell chairs, one manufacturer remembered that his partner used to come back some weeks when he hadn't sold one! 'he left 'em away and gone back Monday to sell them again'. In later years this task of establishing contacts for sale was still the most difficult side of the business. Frank Williams 'Started on me own in my woodhouse, and made dining chairs. Didn't know how to set out to get rid of them, somebody said to me, you go up to Tottenham Court Road, and there I stood on the edge of the pavement and didn't know what to do. I saw a shop, and a Wycombe man came out from the side door, I thought to myself Frank, that's the place for you to go, in that door'. The buyer came out and gave him orders to two sets of oak Queen Anne dining sets, and by going to that shop, it opened up accounts at all other branches in London and the Home County belonging to that firm.

By the 1860's many of the manufacturers had become involved in the export of chairs abroad. C. E. Skull, in reviewing the history of his firm, recalled that in 1865-70 'A great deal of export trade was carried on, principally, I think, to Australia. The goods consisted of cane seated chairs, of varied designs, and they were knocked down to pieces and numbered, and then packed in cases holding three or six dozens each. Also a large trade was done in cane seat and back folding chairs, a chair which is very seldom seen now anywhere else than on board ship, where they are called deck-chairs'.

It is this type of chair which is recommended by Charles Hursthouse in 1861, when compiling his fascinating book on emigration to New Zealand. 'As all articles in the cabin go freight free, passengers often crowd in things till they can scarcely get into bed or get out'. He gives a list of essential furniture and adds 'also provide one or two American easy chairs with cushions for deck use'. This is sensible advice, but it does seem rather frivolous to continue 'I would advise any fair emigrant to take a piano with her as part of her battery of charms!' This aspect of emigration was obviously very dear to the heart of Mr. Hursthouse. 'Bonny lasses who would assist the mistress in the nursery or kitchens as well as active housekeepers might often obtain good situations; and I may perhaps hint to some of my fair readers that the matrimonial market is not overstocked in New Zealand and the statistical facts would appear to indicate the existence of an extensive field for crinoline, red petticoat, Balmoral boot, enterprise and conquest'.

The idea of stocking up the cabin with chairs and other furniture for the life over the water is not a new one. Moll Flanders in the novel by Daniel Defoe written in 1722 recounts that 'We put on board the ship which we went in a large quantity of good furniture for our house, with stores of linen and other necessities' and later when she made a second voyage to Virginia she decided to do so in style. 'I ordered abundance of good things for our comfort in the voyage; brandy, sugar, lemons etc., to make punch, also a larger bed and bedding proportioned for it'. She also considered what else would be needed when she arrived, 'all kinds of house furniture, which, if to be bought in the country, must necessarily cost double the price'. The trade card of Thomas Butler of the Strand, printed in 1800 mentions bedding and furniture 'calculated for the East and West Indies, Ship cabins furnished, articles particularly adapted and made for travelling and exportation'. The reason is made clear in 'Annals of an Anglo-Indian Family' edited by Sir M. Nalcolm, where the writer in 1821 advises his daughters who are about to set forth for India 'Your cabin furniture, if it has no other recommendation, is English, and will always have a value in proportion to your length of absence from England. I have now most of my cabin furniture which I bought in 1811'.

We also tend to identify the export trade with the more recent decades, but in the petition 'Case of the Canechair Makers' of 1680 it seems that 'above two thousand dozens are yearly transported into almost all the Hot Parts of the World'. In 1700 chairs to the value of £7,560.18s.5d. were exported from London and by 1888 this trade had amounted to £746,000 with two thirds of this going to the Commonwealth. As the Art Nouveau and the Arts and Craft Movements in Britain gathered pace, their designs became very popular on the Continent where it was imitated a great deal. J. P. White, writing in 1901, reports that the work of British designers, although not known well in England 'has excited so much interest and met with so much flattering imitation from Continental artists'. So we find a number of firms entering the field of export. In 1902 Thomas Glenister was advertising himself as a wholesale and export chair manufacturer and upholsterer, whilst William Birch of High Wycombe produced much of the 'Quaint' furniture which was popular and could be bought in Austria, France, Germany and Italy. Some of these chairs can be found in the Victoria and Albert Museum, while others are exhibited in the Nordenfjeldske Kunstindustrimuseum in Trondheim as examples of modern industrial design.

Among the nineteenth century Government contracts for export would probably have been the one-arm military chairs, destined for the officers' mess in India, Egypt and other far flung outposts of the Empire. Very few of these can now be found in England, and in William Collins' catalogue of 1862 was the unusual beech and cane chair fitted with four poles, in which natives could carry the sahib or memsahib in the Far East. It would be interesting to know how many of these still survive in the Orient or the wilds of Africa.

Mr. Hussey recalls making chairs at the Wycombe firm of W. E. Ellis, in the form of loose orders, 'the things done loose and for export . . . they used to buy from Ellis, not glued up and in the white'. In view of this trade, it is surprising to read of the Swedish and Danish 'knock-down' or package furniture of the late 1940's referred to by Gordon Logie as a recent innovation. It has since become very popular as the do-it-yourself phase has taken over, and furniture through the post has taken the place of much personal buying. A recent reprint of Heal's Middle Class Furnishing Catalogue 1853-1934 and other similar publications, makes one realise the importance of these catalogues to both manufacturers and to customers in other parts of the globe. It indicates also that the 'modern' assembly of furniture in the home was not uncommon over one hundred years ago.

Chapter Six

THE MACHINE AGE AND THE LAST OF THE BODGERS

When Lord Randolph Churchill referred to the products of High Wycombe as 'cheap and nasty' in the 1870's much indignation was felt in the town, as a statement such as this is very difficult to live down. Unfortunately a similar reference was made in the Sweating Shops' Report of 1888 'the third class work done at Wycombe and Bethnal Green and the East End of London for working men's homes comprising common chairs . . . that is the lowest class of trade'.

So that was the image of Wycombe in the later years of the nineteenth century and one which still occasionally raises its ugly head, even today, when the whole attitude to chairmaking has radically changed. Although the chair industry had been mass-produced from an early date, the use of machinery in the factories was quite a late innovation. 'First and foremost among the pioneers of woodworking machines must be placed Sir Samuel Bentham (1757-1831) whose patents in the years 1791 and 1793 are truly remarkable' writes Manfred Powis Bale in 1880. 'Many of the principles set forth in Bentham's specifications have been the subject of a number of patents during the present century'. He also adds, 'Till within the last thirty years, wood working machinery in this country must be considered to have been in a very crude state, but of later, great impetus has been given by the constant battle between Capital and Labour. The great cost and, in some cases the inferior quality of work turned out by hand, have rendered the increasing introduction of labour saving machinery absolutely necessary, to keep pace with the general progress of the times'.

Even so, the pole-lathe still stood in the corner of the factory when W. O. Haines started work in 1894 and it was in constant use, cutting the tenons for the legs of the Windsor chairs. The introduction of steam power came about 1864 for one manufacturer in Wycombe was listed as a wholesale export chair manufacturer by steam power and steam mills. The first item of machinery introduced in the factory was usually the band-saw which did the cutting out of the back feet etc., and so replaced the up-and-down-saw. This was followed by the round tenoning machine which took the place of some of the work of the pole-lathe, and then

74

The seat hole boring machine which drills two holes at the same time at the required angle to take the legs. This machine brought this task into the range of the semi-skilled man, and naturally speeded up the work considerably. c1890.

This workshop in 1902 shows the overhead shaft and the numerous belts reaching down to the machines on the shop floor. The position of this shaft determined where the machinery would have to stand.

came the boring machine which did away with the tedious job of boring all the holes in the chair seat frames by hand, ready for the caner.

Other machines were introduced such as the seat adzer, the planing machine and the sanders and polishers. All these machines were driven by steam power from belts which were linked to a main shaft running the length of the factory roof to the point where it received power from the steam engine. The belts and shaft determined where the various machines could be placed, also the number of machines which could be safely positioned in the workshop. The introduction of electric power revolutionised the shop floor, as the source of power no longer tied down the machines to their traditional positions. In an article on this topic J. R. Shanley commented 'Get rid of the belt and shaft and you could move machines around like men on a chess board'.

Today the machines are fed automatically and are linked to the conveyor belt, and as the various parts of the chair are joined together, finished off and polished we see the product emerging hardly touched by hand. The factories themselves began to change and the design of these newly built shops had moved away from the narrow wooden structures of the past. Birches of Wycombe were the first to pull down their old buildings and erect 'a fine range of substantial brick three-storey buildings with lift and modern application for heating. Curiously enough this, the first fire-proof factory built in Wycombe, was soon after destroyed by fire'.

Another change came in the range of timbers used. The basis for the chair industry developing in the Chilterns lay in the everlasting supplies of beech, but this supply, contrary to the belief of Daniel Defoe, was drying up, and it was necessary to import timbers, in particular birch, from Canada, to supplement the home-grown wood. One firm, that of W. O. Haines made their own arrangements for timber and over the years they acquired some four hundred acres of woodland. This timber was continually renewed. 'I cut down two hundred trees a year and always plant at least two thousand, principally beech, oak, ash, sycamore and cherry. My father lived to be eighty-four and I suppose in his lifetime he must have planted at least forty thousand trees and he cut down five, and they were only small trees'.

This sense of tradition in ensuring the future of the firm is firmly entrenched in the chair industry, and as change took place in the way the chairs were produced, the greatest change which came was in the quality of the goods manufactured. Charles Skull wrote in 1931 'Whereas at one time Wycombe was noted for one class of goods only, today it is known in

The 'Champion Chair' of the Great Exhibition
of 1851 at Crystal Palace, made by the firm of
Hutchinson's of High Wycombe.

every part of the world as the right place to buy the highest class of chairs, upholstery and cabinet work. Travellers from Wycombe sell all over the Continent, the United States of America, Canada and South America'.

The change seems to have started with the firm of Hutchinson who were turning out the very best class of work in cane-seated chairs. They had scored a signal success with their 'Champion Chair' at the 1851 Great Exhibition. Other firms such as Skull's, Birch's, Janes and North's joined in. The major problem lay in training the men up to the standard to achieve this better class work 'in many cases they were unable to alter their method of work, and in others they flatly refused to have anything to do with work they were not used to . . . our other difficulty was in persuading the leading houses of London that we could make and were making good chairs. I well remember the credulous laugh and the sarcastic remark 'What! Wycombe make anything but cheap chairs?'

The attitude changed when it was realised that the quality work was forthcoming, and in 1884 Skull's were selected to make the presentation chairs for the Prince and Princess of Wales (later Edward VII and Queen Alexandra) and in 1891 they made similar chairs for the wedding of the Duke of York and Princess Mary (King George V and Queen Mary). In an attempt to recapture the spirit of the classical designs, Charles Skull worked from a range of antique chairs which he had acquired and formed into a working collection. About this time Frederick Parker started his collection of seventeenth and eighteenth century chairs and series which was to form the basis for his well-known Parker Collection. He would spend his Saturday mornings visiting antique shops in order to purchase items for reproduction. These would be copied in his workshops, and his firm produced some eighty Chippendale chairs to furnish the liner 'The Ophir' in which the Duke of Cornwall and York (later George V) sailed around the Dominions in 1901. The work had to be carefully done, and the cushions were covered in a fine cream silk which proved too delicate for the factory sewing machines, so this work had to be speedily completed on an ordinary domestic machine. Frederick Parker was awarded a Gold Medal at the Inventor's Exhibition at the Crystal Palace in 1884 for his unusual 'Ambidexter Couch'. On learning that he would have to pay for the award, he politely declined the honour.

To show their chairs off to advantage, local firms opened showrooms in London to attract the desired clientele. Benjamin North had premises in City Road, Keen's in Fitzroy Square area while Birch's kept a showroom and factory combined in Euston Road. This representation in the City was important in order that customers would not imagine the goods they ordered were rural items. The Sweating Shops Commission reports how 'one firm in particular, a West End firm, and old Established firm, have a factory in the country, a customer gives an order there; and this order, instead of being executed in London, is executed at their country factory; but when it comes from the country the factory men have been instructed to see that no sign of any packing whatsoever is left inside or outside of any of the goods, for the very reason that the customer is to believe that it was manufactured in the London factory'.

The firm of Janes followed Hutchinson in getting away from the cane and Windsor chair which was so traditional, and started production on the fashionable black and gilt drawing room chair and the upholstered dining room chair. This was followed by sideboards and tables until a whole range of furniture was achieved. Several firms from Wycombe were represented at the 1881 Furniture Exhibition in London, and Benjamin North exhibited some 'very beautiful rush-seated chairs and a carved satinwood cabinet which was the talk of the whole exhibition'.

Just as these firms were moving their showrooms into London, Parkers were thinking of moving to Wycombe where they had many contacts with the chairmakers. It was when he met Alan Janes at Maples that the suggestion was made of an immediate transfer to premises at Frogmore in Wycombe, a move which was completed in 1898.

About this time Wycombe had entered the age of reproduction which today is as popular as ever, as Pevsner commented 'copying, I was told, is also one of the main sources of supply of the design of Wycombe products' but I feel many customers would agree with John Betjeman who said 'I must confess, too, that I would rather have a well-made fake than an indifferently made piece of modern furniture'. This reviving and copying of eighteenth century furniture called for expert carvers, and the apprenticeship was very thorough. Some of the carvers have created reputations in their own right. Alfred Oakley, after receiving training in a Wycombe chair shop took art training and became a prominent woodcarver and sculptor. Many of his pieces were commissioned and others exhibited at international exhibitions all over the world. Some of his more elaborate carvings were the result of a commission for the panels in the First Class Lounge of the R.M.S. 'Queen Mary' which was launched in 1934, where, to add to the problem of designing the panels, allowance had to be made for five concealed panels which could be opened to reveal film projectors when the Lounge was used as a cinema.

At the present moment Frank Hudson carries on the tradition of producing chairs, furniture, mirror frames and other architectural carvings to a very high standard. He finds 'you mustn't mix the styles today, they've got to be right and in character every time' adding philosophically 'there are more critics today than ever'.

Thomas Glenister at the beginning of the twentieth century supplied a large number of chairs and stools for the Coronation of King Edward VII and this tradition of producing impeccable civic furniture survives today. The chair commissioned in 1947 by Lady Button for the Tower Ward of the City of London was made by Maurice Clark Ltd., from oak taken from the burned and charred beams of the London Guildhall. This chair, although modern in treatment has the traditional lines of the Restoration Armchair of James II. Following the death of A. Graham Doggart, Chairman of the Football Association from 1961-63, his widow commissioned Waring & Gillow to make a chairman's chair in commemoration of his services to soccer. The resulting chair is a massive oak structure, polished to a rich nut colour and upholstered in leather surmounted by the crest of the Football Association, which was designed and manufactured by E. H. Archer of High Wycombe in 1964.

More recent are the three ceremonial chairs presented to the Worshipful Company of Furniture Makers by Lucian R. Ercolani, Chairman of Ercol

Master's Chair designed by Lucian R. Ercolani, O.B.E., and presented with the Warden's Chair to The Worshipful Company of Furniture Makers in 1972. The beautifully designed and produced chairs are made of elm and in the carved panels illustrate tools and the timbers used in making chairs.

Furniture, in 1972. Made of elm they 'represent thought and work over twenty years and are the culmination of the dedicated work of a man who came to this country as an immigrant from Italy in 1890, and has become one of Furniture's best-known figures'. The use of elm arose because of its 'gentle colour and being susceptible to a lovely finish'. Appropriately the lower back panels of the Master's chair contain montages of the basic tools of the furniture maker, carved in bas-relief.

High Wycombe itself has reacted to civic events with real enthusiasm over the years, and when any Royal event or visit has been arranged, pride of place among the bunting and crowns and other decorations has been the traditional arch of chairs which spans the road by the Guildhall. Rising to over thirty feet, it consisted of a solid mass of six or seven hundred chairs surmounted by a row of the large more opulent armchairs on the top.

Together with the change of machinery, design and quality, came new kinds of transport. The horse waggons had lasted well, but new methods had to be used or tried, in order to speed up the transit of chairs. The railway was the obvious answer, but experience had shown its inadequacies, for chairs are light but bulky, rather fragile and cannot be exposed to inclement weather. Complaints had been made in 1874 and 1882 to the Railway Company regarding the accommodation for freight at Wycombe Station. For long journeys it was realised the rail had to be used, but on the shorter trips, mechanised road transport was the answer.

In 1893 a powerful steam traction engine was delivered to Messrs. Plumridge with two timber trailers. Most of the town turned out to see it unloaded at Wycombe Railway Station and follow its triumphant progress through the town. Many more came to watch after it broke the bridge across the River Wye in 1899 and slowly subsided into the mud! In 1904 the firm of William Keen introduced the 'motor trolley', a steam waggon which could carry a load of chairs and pull another loaded trailer behind it. This vehicle now covered the return trip to London in fourteen hours instead of the thirty-six hours required by the horse-drawn waggons, and carried a load of seven hundred chairs into the bargain.

Long after the sawmills and the workshops had machinery to saw the logs into chair legs, the bodger still survived and was able to pursue his craft with profit. A number of chairmakers still felt that the bodger's chair legs were superior and Edward Harman points out it was 'not because of any sentimental reason or to try and keep an ancient craft going, but because it was economic. The old bodgers could turn out chair legs

One of the Civic Arch of Chairs erected by the Guildhall in High Wycombe. This one was built to celebrate the visit of the Prince of Wales (later Edward VII) to Hughenden Manor, home of Benjamin Disraeli in 1880.

The first steam lorry used in Wycombe by Wm. Keen, leaving for London in 1904. The journey took fourteen hours return in comparison with the two days and nights taken by the horse-drawn waggons.

quicker and of far better quality than the best up-to-date automatic machine of that time'.

As the earnings of the factory workers increased, and those of the bodgers stayed at their old level, or even slightly lowered, there was little incentive for newcomers, so the number of bodgers in the Chilterns diminished until by 1940 only a few were actively working in the woods around Wycombe. One of these was Samuel Rockall who lived and worked at Turville Mandeville in the Hambleden area. He made his own drawshave horse in 1896 when he started work. His uncle had preceded him working some thirty years at the same place. Samuel started at the pole-lathe but, as a youth wished to own a wheel-lathe. This was an advanced model in which the foot-treadle motivated a wheel instead of the pole, and that in turn revolved the lathe-shaft. These lathes were comparatively costly and Samuel saved up the six sovereigns which was the current price and in order to learn how to use it he worked for fourteen days with his uncle and they liked the partnership so well that he stayed.

Although the wheel-lathe could be said to be an improvement over the pole-lathe as it rotated continually in the same direction, instead of using the forward and reverse movement of the former, Samuel Rockall found he could only complete two gross of legs on the wheel-lathe against three gross on the pole-lathe. It took practice before he was able to equal his former output. In notes he made for H. J. Massingham, Rockall says 'I do not profess to be a chairmaker although I do make one occasionally and stools of my own design made from cherry wood .. every one that see them are wanting one for themselves, I have got a lot ordered and some of them have to wait over a year before I could manage to get them done'.

The brothers Owen and George Dean were working in the Hampden woods before the Second World War. George extended his experience by going to evening classes in turnery and at the age of twenty-six he left the woods to use a power lathe in a High Wycombe factory. But having worked for some years with his brother he writes with affection of those days 'They were very pleasant to work in, and on the whole, the job was a healthy one, though in the winter one needed to be a bit tough'. The Deans, like Samuel Rockall, came from a family of wood-turners, and their father, Richard Dean had been working in the woods in the later years of the 19th century.

When Adrien Bury wrote his article on Jack Goodchild in 1948, he used the rather fulsome title 'Mr. Goodchild's immortal chairs' and to many people the work of this craftsman is prized and valued in a way unusual

Jack Goodchild in his workshop cutting an intricate Gothic splat for a Windsor chair.

for furniture not considered antique or trendy. Jack Goodchild in his younger days had worked on many types of chairs, but at some point had taught himself to make all the parts of the Windsor, using many local fruit woods. He pursued his craft from turning the legs to framing up the chairs, and his workshop was stacked with chairs in various stages of completion. They were jostled by tools, splats and woodshavings, presenting the picture of a man working among treasured timbers, moving from one chair to another, working as the spirit moved until a final process brought them to completion.

His friend H. J. Massingham waited two years and two months for a Chippendale Windsor chair Goodchild had promised which was fashioned with extra width and strength. As he viewed his completed chair, Massingham wrote 'As I did gaze at this work of superb English craftsmanship, I reflected that I now possessed a chair that expressed a miracle of continuity'.

Although Jack Goodchild worked in a workshop, attached to his cottage at Naphill, and at times used chair legs made by other bodgers, he is still considered the archetype craftsman, bodger and chairmaker, and when he died in 1950, a craft died with him.

Chippendale Bow-back Windsor chair with cabriole legs made by Jack Goodchild and presented to High Wycombe Museum.

When the Second World War finished, those furniture manufacturers who for the past five years had been producing government contracts, were able to turn once again to the task of making chairs. They first saw the introduction of utility furniture, which in making the full use of such timber as was available, created a style which was not pretentious, yet had clean lines and good proportions. During this utility period the Windsor chair made a vigorous recovery and entered into a period of popularity once again.

As the restriction on the supply of timber eased, many chairmakers felt it vital that they should identify themselves with some particular style or design. The increasing popularity of television in conjunction with the press as a medium for advertisement caused innovators such as Ercolani and Gomme to bring out furniture which was made well-known to the public through advertising and which was also easily recognisable by its styling and quality as the work of these manufacturers.

Ercol Furniture Ltd. chose to produce a chair in a Windsor style, yet one which did not imitate the handmade chairs of past decades. Instead they produced chairs, tables and other furniture which caught the spirit of the finer Windsors of the eighteenth century. E. Gomme Ltd., on the other hand, decided to produce a range of fittings in which all the furniture conformed to a pattern, and where the number of variations possible enabled the customer to plan his room to meet personal requirements. This was dubbed the G-Plan. Both these developments depended largely upon long runs and large sales, but time has proved their success.

Just as the belt and shaft had been swept away with the introduction of electric power to create a conveyor belt concept, now we find the machine itself to be the obstacle to future progress. To create a new style of chairs, any firm is involved in months of re-tooling of the machines, which can prove both expensive and lengthy. This expense can only be recouped with long runs, and short runs or 'one-off' orders are often out of the question. A new proposal, which could alter the whole concept of a furniture factory, is known as TTT which stands for Timber Tape Technology. With this the machines to be used have a number of cutting and sawing attachments which can be used in varying positions, and by the use of a specially programmed tape, the chair parts could be moved through the machine, working in a forward, reverse or sideways movement, held in position for a stated time, and the appropriate cutters can be automatically selected and used to create the necessary joint, cut or process. The magnetic tape is the key item, and the use of different tapes produce a different type of work, so a library of such tapes could enable a company to meet a sudden demand or to revive a particular style with the minimum trouble.

This new technology is not mass production, but flow-line production, and in twenty years or so the modern factory we know today will be as obsolete as the nineteenth century timber workshops seem today. This seems a long way from the bodger working in the woods and the chairmaker at his bench, but I suspect alongside these new monuments to a space-age technology, we will still see the older type of workshop which will provide an island of sanity in a world staggering under the burden of computers and time and motion madness.

Part Two: Design and Style

Chapter Seven

THE DESIGN OF THE WINDSOR CHAIR

Whilst there had been early prototypes, the Windsor chairs at the beginning of the eighteenth century appeared in a fairly finished form. Although existing examples may exhibit a variety of minor differences, it seems apparent that the intermediate stages in design which usually herald the development of any new style did not appear or have not survived.

The Windsor chair appears first as a comb-back, taking its name from the strong resemblance to a comb with its top rail and sticks. This top-rail became known as the cresting-rail but more commonly as the comb. Early examples show it shaped very elaborately, bearing a great similarity to the decorated upper rail of the Restoration cane chair of the late seventeenth century. These had a central crown carved on the rail with scrollwork stretching to finials on each side. Such a crown appears on the comb of the 'Barley-Sugar' Windsor chair dated by J. D. C. Ward as c.1680. The barley sugar twist in the middle spindle and lower front stretcher suggests an early example, but the seat is deeply saddled in a way not usual in chairs of this period.

The scrollwork and shell decoration of the Parker-Knoll Collection chair in ash and elm also follows the line of the Stuart pattern, but soon this rather attractive shaping of the comb becomes rather formalised until, with the Bodleian chair of 1766, or the Goldsmith chair of c.1750, it loses most of its decorative effect.

The dating of these chairs is very uncertain, so it is valuable to be able to place some key designs with accuracy. Jackson's Oxford Journal of 1766 notes that 'The Bodleian Library has most confessedly been much improved by the introduction of Windsor chairs so admirably calculated for ornament and repose'. Their elm seats were dished and the remainder of the chair made of ash and it was probably locally made. Like many of the early examples, its legs are shaped with a spokeshave and not turned, nor is there a bracing stretcher.

The Goldsmith chair in the Victoria and Albert Museum originally belonged to the famous writer and acts as a pattern for many other similar chairs of the period. It is dated as mid-eighteenth century and has a round dished seat with a bobtail and back braces. Although earlier than the

Back Bow
Comb or Crest Rail
The Splat
Sticks
Arm Bow
Seat
Saddle
Cabriole Leg
Turned Leg
Knee
Cow-horn Stretcher
H-Stretcher

Comb-Back Windsor
Chair

Bow-Back Windsor
Chair

The Windsor Chair

A fine Comb-back and a Pointed Gothic Windsor in Jack Goodchild's workshop in 1948.

Beautifully designed Windsor Comb-back arm-chair of painted wood bequeathed by Oliver Goldsmith in 1774 to William Hawes, M.D. This style is now called the Goldsmith Chair. *(Victoria and Albert Museum)*.

Unusual bow-back Windsor chair with vase splat, mid 18th century. Note the use of turned legs at the rear, and the front cabriole legs terminate in a 'hoof foot'.

Bodleian comb-back, the legs are turned, and have a more sharply angled splay than most chairs of the period. In this it more resembles the American pattern.

The shape of combs, which included the scroll effect, gradually changed and developed into a stylised curl or carved rosette at the end of a straight rail. In England this was simplified further until a straight rail was achieved, but in America the curve of the comb became strongly emphasised and the scroll effects at the finials curved more and more until they became known as ears. When these were further extended they became horns, and it has been suggested that if carried to an extreme they were so shaped to hang a small 'betty' lamp on the horn to allow the user of the chair to read or sew more comfortably in its light.

With the comb-back chairs, the back supports are usually upright and straight, and it is the alteration of this style which gives us the aptly named fan-back chair. This is most easily distinguished in the side chair, as it shows quite clearly the way in which the sticks fan outwards from the seat into a wider comb. Some American authorities are quite strict in defining a fan-back, not allowing an armchair to be so called when the

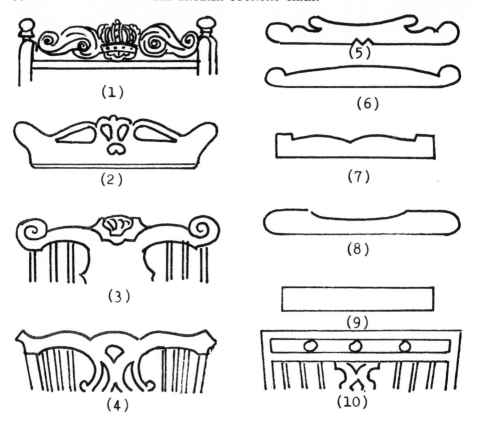

(1) Cresting rail of Restoration Cane Chair c.1680
(2) Comb of the Barley Sugar Windsor Chair c.1680
(3) Comb of Parker Knoll Collection Windsor c.1740
(4) Comb of Chippendale Windsor 1770-1810
(5) Fanbacks c.1750
(6) Comb from the Goldsmith Chair c.1750
(7) Comb from Bodleian fanback single chair c.1770
(8) Comb from Bodleian Library Windsor c.1766
(9) Final form of the comb early Nineteenth Century
(10) Top rail of the Mendlesham Chair c.1820.

Examples of Cresting Rails and Combs found in the Comb-back Windsor Chair.

back rises out of an armbow, insisting that the sticks must rise uninterrupted from the seat. Fortunately, in England we are not so precise. The Bodleian offers a simple fan-back, dated as the second half of the eighteenth century, which still retains vestiges of the crown and scrollwork in its comb and the four simple back supports illustrate very clearly the fan-back shape. So too does the Chippendale fan-back side chair with its comb-cresting and cabriole legs which dates from the same period.

Back braces are found frequently on all types of chairs and they tend to strengthen them. They have not become a standard part of the design as they require a larger piece of timber in order to cut out the bob-tail, and the placing of the bracing sticks in the comb requires skill to ensure the necessary tension is achieved.

A notable change in the Windsor design came with the introduction of the cabriole leg in the 1750's. This takes its name from the French dancing term for a leap or caper. Critics have considered its elaborate shape not well suited to the hard seat line of the Windsor, and decorated leg-brackets were often used to soften and disguise the point where they meet the underside of the seat. This type of leg was used in some areas as early as 1730 when it was designed as a hoof foot with carved fetlocks, a feature surviving from the chairs of 1650-1700, but the date of 1750 is generally assigned to their use on Windsors. Usually only the front legs were shaped, but in some examples all four legs are in cabriole style and appear with or without stretchers. It remained in vogue up to about 1780 after which time it was occasionally in use until 1810. Sometimes it is stated that the cabriole leg ousted the turned leg, but this is doubtful. Following the phasing out of the cabriole the baluster or turned legs were turned with the main swell higher up the leg.

Chairs in varying styles and patterns were being produced at the same time in different parts of the country, making many generalisations unsound. This is borne out by the fact that whilst quite plain chairs may be dated mid-eighteenth century, the Royal Household Accounts for 1729-33 record that Henry Williams, joiner, supplied a 'very neat' mahogany Windsor chair costing £4 for the Prince of Wales' Library at St. James, and that for the Blue Room of St. James, he also made at a cost of £8 two other mahogany Windsor chairs, richly carved.

Looking at the Parker-Knoll Collection Windsor chair it is tempting to see in its decorative splat a development of the carved framework of the central cane panel of the Restoration armchair. This use of the carved back splat or baluster was already becoming a feature of the Windsor

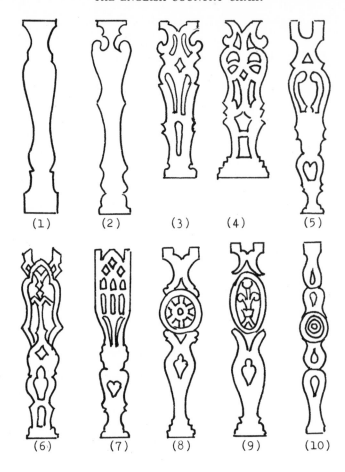

(1)   (2)   (3)   (4)   (5)

(6)   (7)   (8)   (9)   (10)

(1) and (2) early Eighteenth Century unpierced 'vase' splats
(3) Chippendale splat c.1770
(4) Development of Chippendale splat, somewhat later.
(5) Classical Urn or Vase splat c.1770-1820
(6) and (7) Gothic splats c.1750-1770
(8) Wheel back splat c.1820 to date
(9) Prince of Wales Feathers splat c.1790-1830
(10) Blind wheel or disc splat c1820-30.

Splats or Balisters used in Windsor Chairs.

Windsor single bow-back armchair with wheel splat. Early 19th century.

Early comb-back Windsor showing the fiddle back splat, and the comb with shell ornament which strongly resembles the top rail and ornament of the Stuart cane chairs. Note the pronounced 'ears' c.1680 *(Parker-Knoll Collection).*

design, and in many cases it was merely a shaped decorative support. In time however, it was pierced into patterns which included such motifs as the classical urn.

The other basic shape of the Windsor was the bow-back which was in use by the 1740's and it ran parallel with the comb-back form many years before replacing it. The comb-back had for some years used a horizontal bow as a strengthening feature for the arms and back through which the spindles passed. From this it was a short step to introduce a hooped cresting rail or bow as it was called, bringing into the Windsor range the low-back single-bow chair and the more familiar double-bow back.

Although the term used for all chairs of this construction is stickback, this name is usually applied to chairs which do not have a splat. The Americans refer to the English bow-back as a sackback chair. The naming of chair styles is often derivative, so it was not surprising in the eighteenth century to find a Chippendale Windsor. This takes its name from the sweeping curves in the comb and the attractive piercing of the splat which

(Left)

Traditional Windsor wheelback armchair with cabriole stretcher, early 19th century, together with charming bow-back child's chair. mid-19th century.

(Below)

One-arm military Windsor chairs, c.1890 *(right)* lath-back *(left)* scroll. The absence of the left arm allowed the formal dress-sword to hang unimpeded when the officers sat down to dinner in the Mess.

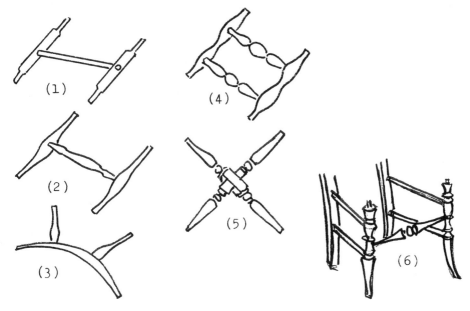

(1) early H-Stretcher, 18th Century.
(2) H-Stretcher - used at all periods.
(3) Cow-horn or Crinoline Stretcher, also
    called spur stretcher.
(4) Double H-Stretcher with 'sausage' turnings
(5) X - Stretcher.
(6) Box Stretcher.

Stretchers or Underframes found in Windsor chairs and Wycombe chairs.

is based on the ribbon motif used in Chippendale chairs. In some instances this motif is quite striking in its similarity to the original design, but frequently it is modified, perhaps to cut down the width of the splat or reduce the amount of piercing required, until there is little difference between it and the stylised urn design. The Chippendale Windsor belongs to the second half of the eighteenth century, from about 1770 into the Regency period, finishing in some districts as late as 1850.

At the same time that the Chippendale was in vogue, a new movement was gathering in English art form, which dedicated itself to the Gothic revival. These designs soon transferred to the Windsor bow-back, and there followed some twenty years during which Windsors were made with few or no sticks, but with large open back supports called window splats. These were designed with a large central, and usually two side splats of similar or complementary motifs. The carving strongly resembles the open tracery of a church window, and the back bow, although often round, frequently copies the pointed shape of a gothic church arch or doorway. These chairs carry such names as 'Strawberry Hill', 'Twickenham' or 'Jemmy', after the originator of the style, Horace Walpole. It also incorporated the cabriole leg with decorated brackets and the chairs were chiefly made of mahogany and other finer woods. Between 1750 and 1780 the curved cow-horn stretcher was introduced, and it was used in many chairs replacing the more familiar H-stretcher. Other names for this cow-horn include crinoline stretcher or spur stretcher; in some instances it was found as a double stretcher with the two curves meeting and joined in the centre of the underframe.

Probably the most attractive example of Gothic Windsor chairs is in the Victoria and Albert Museum. The triple splat armchair echoes the magnificence of the more elaborate excesses of the Gothic revival, and this influence was to be felt through the Regency period into Victorian days, with the interlaced bow and the simpler side chair with its baluster and arch-back rail.

The comb-back went through many phases during the eighteenth century, one very scarce variation was the balloon back in which the comb is shortened to the extent that the sticks curve sharply inwards. One example, illustrated by Marjorie Lidstone and dated c1780 has the rods jointed into a half-circular disc instead of a comb. The Gothic had a vital but short life in the 1760's and so it is reassuring to find that the wheel-back Windsor has scarcely changed in style since its introduction over one hundred and fifty years.

The wheel motif now used in the splat, was preceded by a few true wheel-back chairs in which the circular back actually included in its design the hub and spokes of a large wheel. Once the pierced wheel was accepted, it overtook the more exaggerated patterns and has remained a faithful best seller ever since. At some time an unpierced turned wheel replaced the normal one on a splat. Often called a 'disc', this was around 1820-30, but was not greatly used. Another splat design to achieve popularity was the Prince of Wales feathers. This is usually associated with the eighteenth-century chair designer George Hepplewhite, for he incorporated this familiar royal badge into his chair designs when under the patronage of the Prince of Wales, later George IV. The feathers design largely replaced the earlier Urn design about 1790 and it may well have been used during the period 1810-1820 when the Prince of Wales acted as Prince Regent in place of his father King George III.

Superb Gothic Windsor chair with cabriole legs with shield shaped knees and open brackets each side c.1760-70.

Windsor bow-back side chair with Prince of Wales feather motif in the splat. Early 19th century.

As the Windsor chair enters the field of antiques, it seems sacrilege to find older examples which have been painted, not polished, yet in fact this was the state in which many were originally sold. The reason for this might be a desire to disguise the variety of woods used in making the chair, or, in the case of chairs to be used in the garden, to take advantage of paint as a preservative against the weather. The favourite colour was green, although red and yellow were also popular. The Goldsmith chair of about 1750 is painted in a very dark colour, almost black, but which has been described as green. In America an early finish was in old India red, dark green being next in favour, whilst yellow was often used for children's chairs. The selling of coloured chairs was considered important in the wording of an advertisement of 1787 which described its chairs as being painted. Later chairs, according to J. C. Loudon, writing in 1835, were more frequently stained with diluted sulphuric acid and logwood. The colour was a deep red, not unlike mahogany, and if the wood was oiled and rubbed for a long time with woollen cloths, the veins and shading became pronounced.

The 1939 catalogue of Walter Skull & Sons includes 'two alternative

Fine diamond shape Windsor stool with well turned legs and stretchers.

Round Low Windsor Stool with legs turnings of Wycombe style c.1870.

chairs which are copies of rare renderings of the wheel-back type of chair. Probably in the one case a stay was added long after the chair was made to strengthen it, but we have copied it exactly as we have found it, because it adds charm. Likewise the other chair which has leather strappings interwoven in the sticks of the back'. Obviously the styles were sufficiently popular to warrant inclusion in the catalogue, but they did not create lasting designs.

Often overlooked in the range of furniture is the Windsor stool, which was extensively used in the early nineteenth century. In the accounts houses, banks and offices the high stool was used with the high desk in true Dickensian atmosphere. The low stool was also popular, although few good examples have survived as this type of stool was not considered worthy of a place in museums. The normal Windsor stool had a round top, sometimes with the handgrip cut in the centre of the seat. The top was often not dished and the typical example had the leg turning of the 1870's with the three rings above the vase turning.

An alternative is the square top or the unusual diamond shaped seat in the Rural Studies Museum at Reading which has the Lancashire style leg turning which includes the cup and vase mouldings. The baluster turned stretcher makes this an attractive piece of furniture and the high gloss of the polish adds a reflective glow to the wood.

The classic stool is the three-legged Windsor stool such as the example in High Wycombe Museum. Although dated at 1870, its appearance and turnings are reminiscent of an earlier period and the stools of the 1860's illustrated in the catalogues show much more prosaic turnings. The unusual feature is the symmetrical 'Isle of Man' stretcher which braces the sturdy legs.

Unfortunately furniture does not seem to have the sense of permanence which existed only a few decades ago, and very little that is purchased, especially if for children's use, is looked after and preserved with the idea of 'passing it on' to the next generation. This was not so in the past, for even the nursery furniture remained intact although perhaps unused for many years before being brought out again whenever a new son or grandchild made its appearance.

Most of this furniture was fairly plain, often Windsors of ladder-back, or even basketware, but there have survived over the centuries a number of fine children's chairs which date back to Stuart and even Tudor times. These often give us useful information about styles in use during the period in which they were made. Some seem so very elaborately produced that one wonders which types would have been used in the farmhouse or cottage. We know they had them for an inventory of the house of Richard May of Writtle for 1669 mentioned that the 'Chamber over the Hall' contained a child's chair, while in Edward George's house, a yeoman, also of Writtle was 'one cradle' and a 'child's chair' in the hall.

Jane Toller, writing on the low survival rate of English children's furniture in comparison with that of American children's chairs, believes a social difference in our way of life is the cause. In England the child in the eighteenth century of the middle and upper class was kept in the nursery out of the way until well out of short-coats. These nurseries and schoolrooms were usually furnished with strong but mostly plain furniture.

In the United States of America the child tended to live in with the family and from the number of treasured pieces which have survived, it seems likely that the furniture matched or was at least equal in design and workmanship to that used by their parents.

Again, the change in working conditions in the mid-nineteenth century and the rise of the new-rich did not change the English situation greatly. The era of hand-made furniture was passing, and although the desire to provide attractive things for their children persisted, the machine and mass-produced chairs which were available had not the individuality and craftsmanship of the earlier period.

Astley-Cooper 'Corrective' Chair of painted wood, early 19th century. These chairs were designed to encourage children to sit upright. *(Victoria and Albert Museum).*

Bergere bow Windsor high chair. This chair shows how the use of unmatched parts can produce an ungainly chair.

Many of the surviving chairs are high-chairs, which in some cases are made as a small chair with long legs, in others were small chairs mounted on a high platform or table. From the early nineteenth century there were often Windsor chairs with the splats ornamented with urns, feathers or the wheel motif, similar to the adult versions. A good number of these have survived; wheelbacks, scrollbacks, and many with the 'pot' hole in the seat hidden by a skilfully fitted lid. The long-legged versions were more difficult to design, as the sturdy legs should not out-balance the slender lines of the seat. Many of these show an almost perfect sense of proportion, often the footrails have disappeared, leaving the supporting pegs or even the holes gaping unhappily. The holes bored in the arms also tell their story, for they secured the restraining bar which stopped the struggling infant from hurtling to the ground. At times this beauty of proportion went astray, and the child's high chair shown here with the bergere bow shows how ugly the high chair becomes when chair parts are adapted and not specially made.

By the 1850's, the cane chair was replacing the solid wooden high chair, it was much lighter in weight and the variety of styles was remarkable. The small low chair was popular for the toddler, the child of two to four years of age. These are most interesting to the connoisseur, as they are frequently copies of the styles of the period. There are bow-backs, scroll-backs, buckle-backs, spindle-backs and chairs with solid seats, cane seats, rush seats or upholstered seats, all of which must have delighted the proud father and reassured the devoted mother. I also suspect that 'Grandpapa' played his part in helping the children to ape their elders and betters. For whereas the modern child is supplied by his doting grandparents with a shining new bicycle on his birthday, in the quiet days of a century ago, a comfortable children's chair was probably the most popular gift.

Of course not all children's chairs were comfortable. The eminent anatomist and surgeon, Sir Astley Paston Cooper (1768-1841), President of the College of Surgeons and also Surgeon to the King, brought out around 1800 his corrective chair which gained much favour. It was a very high chair with a straight back having a broad crest rail and two lower broad rails. The legs lared outwards to give the necessary stability and its purpose was to train children to sit upright. Loudon, writing in 1839, adds that it was recommended with the view to prevent 'children from acquiring a habit of leaning forward, or stooping; the upright position of the back affording support when the child is placed at table, and eating, which a sloping backed chair does not'. He adds, in all fairness 'it is proper to observe that some medical men do not approve of these chairs'.

Whether this comment represented the views of many medical men is uncertain, but their popularity was sufficiently great that similar designs appeared in the Wycombe chair catalogues of the 1860's labelled Astley-Cooper chairs.

Another type of high-chair which went through several styles was one locally called 'jump-ups'. These were made up of a small elbow chair fitted to a stand, stool or table to which it was fastened by a thumbscrew. One type used the bergere shape chair and like most of the designs had an adjustable footrest. Sometimes the stool was replaced by a table at which the child could sit when the days of the high chair were over. Such a table is listed in Loudon with a washing bowl. 'The table is made lower than a chair, in order that the nurse may have the more power over the child when she is washing it'!

Chapter Eight

WYCOMBE WINDSORS AND WYCOMBE WHITES

In dating chairs where detailed information is not forthcoming, there is a tendency to choose a convenient date at which a whole group may be placed together. Due to this practice we find with the earlier chairs made at Wycombe, the accepted date for most is c.1850. This date is influenced by the absence of catalogues earlier than 1849, but when the earliest of these is analysed, the variety of styles and the development they exhibit forces me to conclude that they represent several decades of progress. So it is probable that for some models a rather earlier dating could be suggested.

The development of the traditional Windsor chair probably ended with the introduction of the bow-back with the wheel motif. Although a few wheel-backs can be firmly dated as early as 1780, they are usually considered to have been introduced much later, with 1820 as a probable date. The Wycombe Windsor seems to show developments which could place it at the same date. This sudden rush of styles may have been due to a rapid increase in demand and sale, and we find G. R. Porter, when writing of the labourers' houses in 1836 commenting 'we now see, not carpets merely, but many articles of furniture which were formerly in use only among the nobility and gentry'. This theme is echoed by A. J. Taylor, writing primarily about Sheffield, where, in the 1840's, the workmen's houses were 'furnished in a very comfortable manner'.

Noticeable in the pattern books is the production of three main styles, the bow-back, the scroll-back and the lath-back. As the bow-back has been discussed earlier, it is the scroll-back which grows in interest, as it gives us a strong link with the Regency period, and exhibits the attractive lines which are reminiscent of the fashionable eighteenth-century dining room chairs. In the scroll-back armchair the stands, as the uprights of the back are called, are scrolled or curved backwards at the top, just above the joint of the top-rail, the height has been reduced, so it presents a neater and more fashionable piece of furniture than the normal Windsor, without any loss of comfort. As a ladies chair it was made in a slightly slimmer model, and by the use of different yoke-rails such as the Gothic or the twisted scroll, a wide range of chairs was created. The Gothic scroll-back has a

Scroll-back Windsor armchair, mid-19th century. The elegant design and carved yoke show Regency influence.

The Scroll-back side chair was popular in the mid to late 19th century. *(left)* Gothic Scroll-back. *(right)* Plain wood seat Scroll-back. *(High Wycombe Museum)*

broad back-rail in which four arches are cut and supported by three turned spindles which act as miniature pillars.

The creation of that holy of holies, the Victoria 'parlour' with its museum-like appearance increased the demand for side or single chairs. These were made with solid or cane seats, and we are fortunate in having a number of mid-nineteenth century catalogues to see for ourselves the full range which was available. In many cases they were matched to small armchairs which tend to be called carvers. This term was introduced in the mid-nineteenth century to distinguish between the dining room armchair which was set at the head of the table and the elbow chair found elsewhere in the house.

Lath and Baluster Back Windsor armchair in beech c.1890.

The scroll-back received further fashioning at the hands of Stephen Hazell, who was a maker of Windsor garden and cane chairs in Oxford about 1846-69. His chairs are recognisable by the way in which the arms curve downwards towards the seat, being linked to it by a turned spindle. This is very similar to the line of the Shereton arm, and it soon became a feature in the catalogue of other manufacturers.

As a government contract chair, the scroll-back was popular, and in a very plain economy model was also to be seen in many a club or barbers' saloon. It appears most satisfactory as a side chair, but with the addition of widely splayed arms it becomes an attractive small elbow chair. The Gothic style appears in catalogues of 1849 but its first appearance in print is in Loudon's 'Encyclopaedia' where it is described as a very comfortable and cheap chair.

Perhaps the most significant style which evolved over these years was the lath-back. This is a very heavy chair which puts the Lancashire chair to shame. The housemaid cleaning a floor which involved moving many of these would have real cause to curse their makers. The first chair in the series was a simple stick-back in which the sticks or rods were tapered at each end and secured at the top into a large shaped comb. There was no arm bow as the arms were mortised into the stout outside stands which were slightly turned.

At first the turning in these chairs was plain and limited to the rather stumpy legs and the stretchers. Then the double-H stretcher with its double swell cross-member was used and in time the spindles were made thicker and turned to a pattern to produce a style known as the Roman Spindle.

The next development was made to give more comfort. As the sticks or turned spindles made little allowance for the shape of the human spine, curved laths were introduced, which, being of a rectangular section, rather than round, could be cut into a more reposeful shape. This fitted the small of the back without any loss of strength and became known as the lath-back. Before long, however, its unaesthetic plainness offended the customers and the decorative splay was re-introduced to add the Lath and Baluster armchair to the series.

This popular model lasted for over seventy years in the catalogues, and variations included chairs with personal monograms in the splats, rockers, and the one-arm editions for the use of the army. The most common of the smaller Windsors was simply called the 'wood seat armchair', it has no frills but was a best seller for many a long year. This is also something akin to the ladder-back in the 'plain splat highback armchair' that was in production c.1870-1900. This started off as a scrollback with a very high rail, and to fill in the back, three horizontal splats were fitted instead of the usual single yoke.

The popularity of the scrollback as a low chair probably influenced the introduction of the smoker's bow, which dates from about 1830. In America this type of Windsor developed from the Philadelphia lowback which was current c.1740-80. The English version, whilst it may have been influenced by the American chair, developed independently, possibly with some help from the Lancashire Windsor which it can be seen to strongly resemble. Among the earliest examples of the English lowback is the mahogany baluster back library chair in the Victoria and Albert Museum which is dated c.1780. It has cabriole legs front and back and these, like the back scroll, is finely carved. In place of the spindles are slender fluted columns, and the seat is deeply saddled, a truly noble forerunner of the smoker's bow.

The feature of these chairs lies in the continuous line of the back and armbow which is supported above the seat by up to seven turned spindles. Arising from the bow at the back is a heavy curved crest or scroll. Such was the success of the early design, that it has retained the basic pattern

Mahogany baluster back 'smoker's bow' type library chair c.1780. Note the crisp carving on the back, arm stays and the knees, and use of four cabriole legs. *(Victoria and Albert Museum)*

right up to the 1930's when it gradually lost favour in the public buildings where it had previously been so popular. In 1901 during the Art Nouveau Period, Birches of High Wycombe revived the smoker's bow with added flourishes. The design used laths instead of the normal spindles and this elegant model was marketed at £1.6.3d under the trade name of the Maidenhead smoker. Following the Second World War it has again been produced often with the bow set lower above the seat, only about nine inches at the most, and it is used frequently in restaurants and public houses. Recently passing an open air furniture display by the road in Wendover, Bucks, a splash of colour was provided by a row of neat smoker's bow armchairs, stained or painted red, green, brown and yellow, which really completed the circle.

Another favourite form of the smoker's bow was made by changing the arm bow to a design called a Berger Bow or Bergere which was produced c.1840-80. This chair takes its name from the more conventional bergere, a form of half-couch which it little resembles. The design is rather florid, and the straight bow of the smoker is replaced by a high curve generally supported by wooden splats instead of the more usual turned spindles. As a desk and office chair it was in great demand, and it had even more potential when made as a revolving chair. Both the berger and the smoker were made with wooden, cane or upholstered seats and in time they became the most common office chair.

The berger is typical of the Victorian tendency for curves and comfort, for there is not a straight line to be found in these chairs, and this constant rounding off has created out of the more classical dining room chair of the past, the most common form of Victorian chair, the popular balloon back.

This name was applied to a wide variety of slender chairs made in beech and birch which were generally supplied with cane seat made from the 1820's onwards. They were also known as fancy or chamber chairs and the interest lies in the Victorian tendency to give a name to each variety. The catalogues offer a bewildering collection of chair, including such models as the Quaker chair, the Caxton and the Oxford. Other names are derived from the shapes, such as the Double C and the Crown Back whilst the Rise and Fall back chair is more recognisable as the Kidney Back while the Table Top seems to be another almost Regency style side chair. These names are most descriptive and once introduced to the chair by name, they are not easily forgotten.   This balloon back is not of course a Windsor chair, and so is usually known as a Wycombe chair. These were elegant little pieces of furniture, with the front legs beautifully slender

Double-C Balloon back cane seated Wycombe Chair c.1860. *(High Wycombe Museum)*

Child's scroll-back rocking chair of elm made in 1851. These are included as rockers in the 1872 Wm. Collins Catalogue. *(Victoria and Albert Museum)*

with the feet splayed out in what was termed 'best fore foot' fashion. As Wycombe whites they were often sold ready to be polished or painted, but frequently they would be grained to resemble rose wood or enamelled black, or even painted a combination of colours with floral patterns added in attractive tints. From the crudest ornament, which might be that of a sharp nail dragged in straight lines across the surface of the wood, to the finest of painted chairs, they were so designed that most of the chair parts could be mass-produced to a standard pattern regardless of style until it was decided which chair it was necessary to assemble.

Some earlier models are shown in Loudon's 'Encyclopedia' of 1839 with an additional decorative motif in the centre of the yoke and which are called buckle backs. These were criticised by Loudon as the back legs, which were 'bald', contrasted strongly with the elaborately turned and carved front legs. Another chair which has a rash of twisted cane is also shown, and this tyle appears in the later catalogues under the heading of Swiss chairs.

This tendency for curviness which is exhibited in the balloon back, was not always appreciated by the supporters of the new Gothic Revival.

Writing in the Art Journal in 1867, one contributor felt 'I can scarcely imagine a task more agreeable to a gentleman of means, taste and leisure than to set himself to the consistent decoration and furnishing of the Gothic Villa'. This comment was made only ten years after the Great Exhibition which took place in the great Crystal Palace. Here the Wycombe chairmaking firm of Edmund Hutchinson submitted a truly regal example of Gothic design which was dully dubbed the 'Champion Chair'. The carving on the back incorporates lions, the English rose, the thistle, daffodils, crowns and all manner of other ornament, the upholstery is in crimson velvet and the framework includes enough prickly protrusions to keep the most drowsy chairman alert! Perhaps it was such a chair that prompted another comment in the 'Building News' of 1867 'we want chairs not states or thrones, tables not banqueting boards'.

The influence of these exhibitions was considerable, at the 1862 International Exhibition in London a favourite sculpture depicted a young girl seated on a simple rush-bottomed chair. At once this type of chair, which hitherto had been much too crude for town use, became fashionable in great demand. Trends of this nature could make quite a difference to the chairmaking industry. Sometimes a medical reason with a suitable recommendation from a well-known surgeon or doctor, could popularise a style of chair in the same way that patent medicines become firm favourites.

One example of this was the Astley-Cooper corrective chair which is described earlier, but equally interesting is the 'digestive' chair which was strongly advocated by Dr. Calvert for invalids, members of the weaker sex, and nursing mothers who would find them a boon! Exactly who Dr. Calvers was is uncertain, the honour rests between George Calvert (1795-1825) a surgeon and anatomist, and the chemist Frederick C. Calvert (1819-1873) who among other things was responsible for the early manufacture of carbolic acid and its use as a disinfectant.

Surprisingly enough, this digestive chair turns out to be the rocking chair, invented, if that is the correct word, in America in the 1760's. Benjamin Franklin is reputed to be the first to use one, but it was about 1820 before the 'Boston Rocker' swept the American market and established itself a firm favourite. Its popularity was so great that when Harriet Martineau wrote in 1838 of her visit to America, her strongest impression was of the small inns in which 'the disagreeable practice of rocking in the chair is seen in its excess. In the inn parlors are three or four rocking chairs in which sit ladies who are vibrating in different directions and at various velocities, so as to try the head of the stranger'.

She adds forbiddingly 'How this lazy and ungraceful indulgence ever became general I cannot imagine'.

In England, according to John Gloag, it was not socially acceptable, and it was only on medical grounds that its use was condoned. The early rocking-chairs were usually made by adding rockers to chairs made in an existing range, so we find a number of Windsors and ladder-backs in the catalogues are shown with and without rockers. Indeed the practice of adding the curved sections on a 'while-you-wait' principle was common practice in Wycombe until a fairly recent date.

Probably the first chair to be designed primarily as a rocking chair was made by a new revolutionary method. This was achieved by the Austrian designer Michael Thonet (1796-1871) who in the mid-nineteenth century introduced this entirely new design in bentwood, steamed into shape in his factory in Vienna. The timber, bent along its length was very strong and flexible and it could be so shaped that the rockers became an integral part of the chair. Not surprisingly these new chairs sold well, much to the annoyance of the traditional chairmaker.

John Mayes writes of the real fears in the 1880's and the 1890's of this 'dangerous invader' which was 'not an especially cheap chair nor remarkable for strength and durability, but it was something different!' He adds that although it was a strong rival, no real attempt to copy it was made in Wycombe, instead an all-out attempt to lower prices was made in order to increase the competition. This was so successful that cane and rush seated chairs which fifteen years earlier had sold for fourteen shillings a bundle of six, were now selling at prices between eight shillings and twelve shillings a bundle of six.

This concern was also shown in evidence given at the Sweating Systems Committee in 1888. 'I do not think that public offices ought to be furnished with furniture which they have got from abroad. The bentwood chairs, such as we get from Austria for instance, are ordered by the Office of Works from a maker in Austria . . . I think that in a place like this (The House of Lords) if they do want to furnish it, they ought to do it with furniture made by British workmen'. He rather slyly added, 'I understand the civil servants complain very bitterly about this; that they used to have proper chairs to sit on, and now they do not'.

Another medical aid which is shown in the trade cards and listed as a garden machine appears to be an invalid chair. Lock'n Foulger in 1773 illustrated a simple comb-back Windsor chair mounted on a platform with small wheels and equipped with a steering rod at the front in the style of the old-fashioned bath chair. Probably these wheelchairs would have been seen on the promenades of the new bathing resorts such as Brighton, Weymouth and Southend, which were attracting the public for pleasure as well as health reasons, following the example set by the Prince Regent.

As means of transport advanced and the transatlantic voyages to America become common, the six-legged folding chair with its canework panels or waved slatted back and seat would be seen on deck in the sun, or folded up and lashed down against the storms on the pleasure decks of the cross Atlantic vessels. This folding chair, which is based on the Glastonbury chair, had been formerly marketed as the Derby Chair, but as it was more extensively used on the liners, it became known as the Steamer Chair and eventually as the deck chair. This particular style had greater stability than the usual folding chair as the seat and back were supported by the cross back legs, and the arms as they extended forward joined another upright which both supported and steadied the front part of the seat. The cane folding chair appears in many designs in the catalogues, sometimes painted and decorated in elaborate ornament, other times with accessories such as the bookrest which was hinged and moved in all directions. This folding chair was also in use on the verandah and in the garden, and now with the wood replaced largely by metal and the canework by bright canvas, forms an important part in our leisure life.

Chapter Nine

REGIONAL WINDSOR CHAIRS, LADDERBACKS
AND SPINDLEBACK CHAIRS

Although Windsor chairs of traditional design were made in several parts of the country, some definite regional characteristics evolved which are of considerable interest. The first type is the Cardiganshire chair from North Wales. In 'Welsh life in the 18th century' the authors calculate that Wales was at times one hundred years behind England in some phases of its development. Not until the Napoleonic Wars, when the English visitors came to Wales instead of the Continent, which was closed to them, did ideas and styles change to any great extent. The Cardigan chair has very ancient origins yet the design is that of a low-back Windsor and it bears a strong resemblance to the crude three-legged prototype chair at St. Cross Hospital. This tradition of three legged chairs in Wales is long, for in the Peniarth Manuscript of 1180, we see the Judge of the Court seated on a similar style arm-chair.

The chair was developed with three legs to give stability on the uneven stone floors of the cottage or farmhouse. The construction included a plank seat made of elm or bog-oak of considerable thickness and weight and roughly cut into a semi-circular shape. This curved line is followed in the equally heavy looking arm and back bow with its outward curling ends very similar to the nineteenth century smoker's bow. The spindles, which were all of the same thickness were rather stout and had a single ring turning, half-way up. These were made of birch or beech and were jointed through the seat, protruding slightly underneath. The chairs date from the eighteenth century, and from the same period comes a four legged Windsor with a bow and a very low comb surmounting it. One other style of comb-back attributed to Wales has the sticks bowed inwards and capped by a very small cresting. Fred Roe feels this indicates a local attempt to copy the bow-back without utilising the retaining hoop or bow of the bow-back chair.

The East Anglian chair appeared in tbe early days of the nineteenth century and is often known as the Mendlesham or Dan Day chair. It is a comfortable variant of the low-back Windsor arm-chair, constructed in the

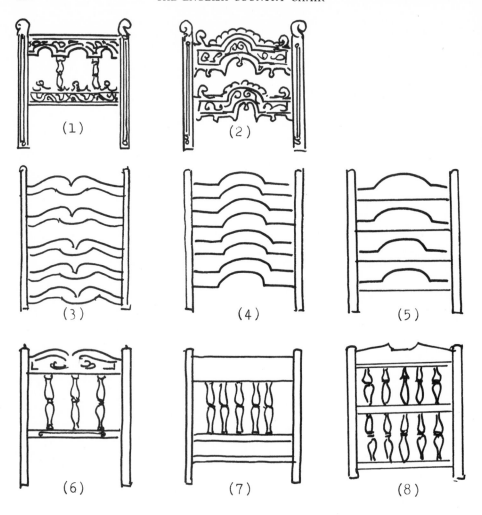

1.   Derbyshire Back chair c.1660.
2.   Yorkshire Back chair c.1660.
3.& 4.   Lancashire ladderbacks 18th Century.
5.   Ernest Gimson's ladderback 19th Century.
6.   Spindle back - linked with Cumberland.
7.   Spindle back - Lancashire type
8.   Spindle back - Yorkshire type.

Some of the so-called regional types of chairs. Opinions vary as to which is connected to each part of the country.

Mendlesham armchair of turned elm, early 19th century. *(Victoria and Albert Museum).*

A Lancashire Windsor chair of yew and elm with cow-horn stretcher and stylized vase splat. Also called a Yorkshire Windsor.

same style, but a noticeable difference is the square finish of the back-rail, which does not resemble a comb or bow in any way.

The chair probably originated in the village of Mendlesham in Suffolk, where the local wheelwright and chairmaker, Daniel Day, commenced making chairs in this particular style. According to William Hatfield, Daniel Day's son is reputed to have worked in Thomas Shereton's workshops, and about 1790 returned to join forces with his father. If this is the case, then this would account for the stylish line of the Mendleshem chair, although some years must have elapsed before it evolved, as it was the beginning of the nineteenth century before most existing chairs were made.

These are usually made in yew or fruitwood, and like the Windsor they have an elm, saddled seat. The legs splay outwards and the arms, which are flat, have sloping supports and follow the same angle. The back includes an almost Regency style copy of the ornamental splat with three sloping sticks each side. This is surmounted by a double crest rail of square section in place of the turned member of the Windsor, and this panel is usually infilled with three turned wooden balls. This feature is sometimes repeated below the splat panel, or may be replaced by a horizontal bow, linked with two turned balls to the cross rail. Most Mendleshams follow the basic pattern with few variations, and the majority of surviving examples are elbow chairs with single or side chairs being rather scarce. This style of Windsor is also linked with Scole in Norfolk, and some authorities tend to use the various names indiscriminately.

Both the Cardigan and the Mendlesham Chair represent true regional varieties in manufacture and style. The Lancashire Windsor, or Yorkshire, as it is also called, is a different matter. Although it is probable that the early eighteenth century chairs of this pattern were made in the northern counties, from the early or mid nineteenth century the design became a standard model in the pattern books of many other chair producing areas.

The Lancashire is more sturdily constructed than the normal Windsor, and it will be noticed that the turnings of the legs, arms and stretchers are also considerably heavier, and it has been suggested, almost to the point of bad taste. But this might be said to be a feature of the Northern style of furniture.

In a lighter vein, it has been said that the hard-headed businessman, determined to get the best return for his money, did not consider simple classical line to be good value. The chair travellers, showing him the pattern books containing these heavier styles, adorned with double swell 'sausage' stretchers, tripple ring and cup turnings on the legs, seem to be offering a much more satisfactory model.

The basic shape differs from the classic line of the traditional wheelback, and it bears a strong resemblance to the low-back Windsor, but has a bow and sticks added above the arm-bow. These sticks frequently do not pierce the arm-bow and enter the seat, instead they are replaced by turned arm supports which match the line of the splat. Some models do have the sticks piercing the arm-bow, but in general the true Lancashire uses the spindles. Although some of the original northern chairs may have come south, most of the Lancashires found in the Home Counties tend to be dated 1820-40 and they were more often made locally. After this period these heavier turnings which are more usually applied to the larger lath-back chair became accepted and more popular and were successfully made in the Chilterns for the London market.

The Lancashire and Yorkshire are names which are really inter-changeable, and indeed to some not even acceptable. But the style was popular in Inn parlours and public rooms. They are usually made almost entirely of yew with just the elm seat and many seem to have been originally varnished, and they survive with a high and transparent gloss on the wood.

A final type of regional Windsor appears in an article by J. D. U. Ward in which he creates a group which he calls the Cotswold Chair, terming them also Shepherd chairs. He refers to them as having a 'rather gawky graceless aspect' and mentions that the seats, which are rather wide, are deeply bottomed. The five chairs he illustrates are all comb-backs but of such varying styles as to make it difficult to easily see a common bond which distinguishes them from other country made eighteenth-century comb-backs.

Our knowledge of the primitive and medieval chairs which were forerunners of the rural chairs is largely based on examples in paintings, sculptures and manuscripts of the pre-reformation days. And whilst many of these early chairs seem to be the solid joined chair similar to the Coronation Chair in Westminster Abbey, some examples bear a striking resemblance to chairs of a much later period.

One of the earliest examples of a turned chair appears in a carving at Chartres Cathedral, which is twelfth century, and it shows a scribe sat at his sloped desk in chair made of heavily turned uprights decorated with simple inscribed ring markings. The front legs extend up beyond the seat to carry the wooden arm, and these are surmounted by a ball finial. The back of the chair is not shown, but between the arms and the seat are six turned spindles behind which an arched effect is shown.

The main structure is very reminiscent of the Carver or Brewster chair of Puritan America. Edward Joy in a recent publication includes an illustration of a Scandinavian chair with turned legs and back which he dates as c.1200. It is referred to as a survivor of the period and as such is a remarkable find. It has ball and ring turnings and finials on all posts and two turned spindles are shown in the drawing below the seat linked to the back stretcher. These chairs have a strong architectural spirit in their design, which is emphasised with the use of pillar effects, archways and elaborate pinnacles or finials.

At some point the turner making these chairs changed the main shape of the framework, basing it on a triangular seat instead of the more usual square. This could not have been a change for comfort as this shape is less roomy and the arm supports are not strategically placed. It was most probably for stylistic reasons, as the increased use of turning and bobbins could have created an overwhelming effect, and the change of line carried the eye directly to the back decoration and the ornaments which

Magnificent thrown chair, of ash and oak and of West Country origin, early 17th century. The ultimate development from the simple triangular stool. *(Victoria and Albert Museum)*

Spindle armchair of oak with the panel in the back carved with dragons interlaced, probably Welsh (Severn Valley) late 16th to early 17th century.

consisted of patterns cut on the lathe before the parts were socketed together.

This type of chair is sometimes called a 'thrown' chair, and is a bobbin chair, in early household inventories it is often included as a 'tourneyed' chair. The amount of decoration varies from chair to chair, from the simple triangular shape with the back leg extended to form a back and topped with a plain crossbar, through to the more developed chair in the Ashmolean Museum which is believed to be East Anglian c.1600, to the peak of craftsmanship which is exhibited in the magnificent early 17th century chairs in the Victoria and Albert Museum. This is stated in the catalogues to be an 'archaic type from Scandinavia, probably of Byzantine origin' but Iorwerth Peate disagrees, 'various theories have been adduced concerning the origins of this type, the least likely is that it is of Scandinavian origin'.

Both of these chairs have very vigorous bobbin turnings, and from Wales comes another thrown chair of equal importance. It is made of turned oak and has a square seat, and it is dated as c.1550. This chair comes from Tregib, Carmarthenshire and is known locally as the 'Justices chair', yet the turnings bear a strong resemblance to those at the Victoria and Albert Museum. Although this style of chair is of great antiquity, it was made well into the 17th century. John Gloag feels that in these bobbin turnings, the turner prolonged the life of native style chairs until the Windsor took over in the late 17th century.

Following the Restoration Period, the back-stool or back-chair as it is also called, completed its metamorphosis from the stool into the side chair which in the eighteenth century was to reach its highest point of excellence. In the seventeenth century, however, early types gradually broke down into three or four main styles known as Lancashire, Yorkshire or Derbyshire chairs.

The Yorkshire was a sturdy oak chair with an open back in which were inserted two arched horizontal rails. The decoration consisted of interwoven scrolls in half relief with finials and suspended below the rails. This was the forerunner of the ladderback. Its companion was the Derbyshire chair in which the two horizontal rails are straight with the upper rail arcaded and joined to the lower rail by two turned spindles. This chair set the pattern for the later spindle backs. In some instances these chairs have come to be called 'mortuary' chairs, due to the inclusion in the design of a death mask of Charles I, presumably as an expression of loyalty.

The spindle chair *par excellence* of the period is typified in the armchair which comes from the Severn Valley and is dated late sixteenth century to early seventeenth century. The panel in the back is carved with interlaced dragons in light relief and this surmounts a row of spindles which continue each side under the armrails. The early eighteenth century development retains this basic shape but inserts a second or third row of spindles to replace the panel. Chairs with an excess of spindles are associated with Lancashire and the North of England. One such chair made in a large size to 'enable our forefathers to repose comfortably therein after an evening's carouse' is called the 'drunkard's chair', a name probably dubbed in the nineteenth century. A more attractive name for this wide seat, which later became a settee, was the Darby and Joan chair. This term stems from a poem written in 1738 and printed in the 'Gentleman's Magazine' which refers somewhat senmentally to 'Old Derby with Joan by his side'.

A much simpler design which survived through the nineteenth century used only three spindles which linked the back rails with a third back rail above. The legs of this rush-seated chair are thick and terminate in a turning known as a 'hoof' foot, which in the nineteenth century chair was made more slender and called best fore foot.

At the same time the ladderback was developed, taking advantage of

A Gimson style rush-seated ladderback, designed by E. W. Gimson in 1904 and is in current production by Neville Neal of Stockton.

18th century rush-seated ladderback chair, the front legs turned to resemble the cabriole leg. *(High Wycombe Museum)*

the new materials and techniques which filtered through to the village chairmakers. The early ladderback is represented in a document dated c.1338-44 in the Bodleian which illustrated a schoolmaster seated at a ladder armchair reading with his pupils. Except for the use of the cross slats below the seat level, there is little difference between this chair and those of the nineteenth century.

We have seen that the Yorkshire backchair gives us the start of the ladderback, this is mentioned because there is little evidence of the use or survival of ladderbacks in the four centuries which span the 'schoolmaster' to the Restoration. The true ladderback was revived as a rushback chair in the seventeenth century in the low countries, hence its name in England as the 'Dutch chair'. A copper engraving of a chair-leg turner by the Dutch engraver Jan Joris Van Vliet who was born in Delft in 1610 shows a good example of a turned ladderback, which doesn't differ greatly from those of a century later.

A ladderback rush-seated armchair with cupid-bow slats, called the Clisset. Produced by Neville Neal of Stockton.

The horizontal slats at this period show many variations but are often a plain lunette shape and the legs have a turning which crudely resembles the cabriole leg. William Old and John Ody in 1720 'makes and sells all sorts of cane and Dutch chairs' in St. Paul's Church Yard. The Lancashire Ladderback which was popular from the mid-eighteenth century was decorated with five or six slats of serpentine shape.

As the chair designers of the mid-eighteenth century looked around for new ideas, the ladderback became respectable and the serpentine shape was adapted in mahogany with pierced slats. As with other designs of the 1770's the elaborate ladderbacks of the drawing room had pierced geometric shapes which show the influence of the Gothic revival, so it is with considerable pleasure I can turn to a well thumbed copy of Dickens' 'Tale of Two Cities' and see the simple and plain ladderback in use again in the wine shops of the 'Phiz' drawings, and find them once again in the

Wycombe Chair broadsheets of the 1860's hidden under the heading of church seats.

There had always been a time-lag of several years between the use of new designs in the Metropolis and their adoption in the provinces, and bearing in mind the present might and advancement of the United States of America, it may seem strange to realise that for many in England in the seventeenth & eighteenth century, the new colonies of Virginia and New England and their successors were as close as some counties in the homeland. Of course ideas and designs took some time to cross the Atlantic but other factors influenced the furniture styles in the new countries.

J. L. Oliver writes that 'New ideas and skills brought from Europe were applied by the sustained efforts and enterprise of well disciplined family, racial and religious communities. Conspicuous among the last were the Quakers who founded the State of Pennsylvania and from the Puritan area of New England, emerges the bobbin-turned chairs of the mid-seventeenth century.

When the first immigrants travelled to America in the early seventeenth century, their ships were very small, and in consequence there was little room for the passengers themselves let alone a cabin full of furniture. So the chairs and tables which graced the first log cabins in these new colonies must have been crude indeed. Originally goods exported to these new colonies were subject to customs duties, but when the Virginia charter of 1606 was drawn up, it permitted the shipment to Virginia of all commodities which were necessary to support life. And so when the New England Charter was also written in 1620 it made allowance for the provision, free of customs duty, of weapons, victual, utensils, furniture, cattle, horses and other things 'necessary for ye sd planacon, & for their use & defense & for trade wth the people there'.

Very little has survived from those pioneering days, for the fight for survival was far more important than furnishing for comfort. When the Mayflower finally sailed from Plymouth, on board was John Alden who came from Essex, and it is he who has the honour of being associated with the earliest furniture of the new colonies. The first identifiable piece of furniture, however, is by another Essex man, a carved chest bearing the inscription 'Mary Allyn's Chistt Cutte and Joyned by Nicholas Disbrowe'. Nicholas was born in Saffron Walden, the son of a woodjoiner, one of many immigrants who came from East Anglia, an area noted for the excellence of this turned woodwork.

By the mid seventeenth century, life in the colonies had become established, and the standard of living had risen to the extent that some luxuries and comforts crept into the timber houses which were being built to replace the earlier homesteads. The earliest types of chairs to emerge as an identifiable style were the Carver and the Bewster chair which bear the names of two prominent New England leaders.

The Carver armchair is attributed to John Carver (1575-1621) born in England and one of the group at Leydon who crossed in the Mayflower in 1620. Bradford's history of the colony records 'After this they chose, or rather confirmed Mr. John Carver (a man Godly and well approved amongst them) the Governor for that year'. The chairs which bear his name and dated c.1660-1700, are usually made of maple, ash or hickory with rush seats. The turned front legs rise above the seat to form the arm supports and the back legs extend to become the frame posts for the back. Two turned horizontal rails in the back are linked by three or more vertical spindles and this unit is surmounted by another turned vase and ring rail. The back posts have steeple turned finials, and one or two arm rails join the back uprights and front arm supports, a simple box stretcher is used for the underframe.

We tend to identify the Carver with the United States alone but it was most probably a style which existed formerly in England and was popular enough to be used as a pattern for children's chairs. In the Victoria and Albert Museum is a child's chair of turned ash with a rush seat dated seventeenth century which is a charming example of this attractive style, although the legs and the turnings and finials have not been scaled down sufficiently to be aesthetically correct.

The Brewster chair is named after William Brewster (1567-1643) an Elder of the Plymouth Community who was also one of the original Pilgrim Fathers. The earliest example of this chair was the property of Governor Bradford (d.1657) who was appointed in 1621 following the death of John Carver who had come in from the fields 'very sick, it being a hot day; he complained greatly of his head and lay down, and within a few hours his senses failed so as he never spoke once more until he died . . . he was buried in the best manner they could, with some volleys of shot by all that bore arms'.

This type of chair is more elaborate than the Carver although built on the same lines. The main difference lies in the considerable increase in the amount of turned bobbin work. The single row of spindles in the Carver chair is replaced with two rows, the lower one has the spindles extending into the back rail. The front stretchers are turned and two rows of spindles extend along the front of the seat almost touching the ground.

Beneath each arm extending down below the seat level on each side are further rows of spindles.

Although the decoration is different the basic shape remains the same and these two chairs are joined by the slatback or ladderback as we know it. These were made over a much longer period of time, but their early phase was c.1680-1710. In this period three slats were used and made in various shapes. The most common slat was a straight wide rail with a bold quarter circle cut out at each end on the upper side. This reduces the tenons to half size so strengthening the uprights and adds a decorative feature to the chair. The front and rear legs are slightly turned with the front legs terminating in a ball finial, these sturdy legs could be anything up to four inches in diameter. The arms were socketed into the arm support below the finial. In later slatback chairs the diameter of the legs was reduced to two inches, making a less stocky chair, the arms no longer joined the front support below the finial, but curved over them forming a handgrip. The stretchers lose their plainness and are turned with ring and ball mouldings whilst the legs now terminate in a small ball or knob foot.

The wide range of immigrants brought craftsmen in from many nations, and each introduced some aspect of his native culture. One or two such styles of furniture have emerged to be accepted and recognised as separate categories. Perhaps the most interesting range is linked with the sect of Shakers who started their first community on the Hudson Bay in 1779. The group was founded by Mother Ann Lee who came from England in 1774, having a spiritual affinity with the Quakers' philosophy. Mother Ann propounded a creed which included the confession of sin, community of goods, celibacy and the withdrawal from the sinful world. Their belief was based on 'dedication of their Hearts to God and the hands to work' and their name arises from the rythmical dance in which the gift of prophecy is believed to come through this agitation of the body.

In 1789 the community of New Lebanon of New York began to specialise in making chairs, and the following years saw the Shakers peddling their wares along the Hudson Valley in the surrounding villages and towns and they also created the first systematic production of slat-back rocking chairs. The Shakers avoided ornament of any type and their furniture exhibits a 'distinctive character because of its utter simplicity'. Although ornamentation was not used, the Shakers did not mind colour and the chairs were grained or painted in red, orange, yellow and brown.

The earliest production of chairs before 1850 by the Shakers was confined to the slatback, but after this date, due to a re-organisation of chair production within the Community, the major proportion of chair made for sale were slatback rockers. The chairs, whether rockers or not, usually had three plain slats, straight on the lower edge and curved on the upper. Although the Shakers have always offered seats in cane, rush, upholstered or woven in fabric tape. The latter style seems to have been the overwhelming favourite. At first this was woven from home-grown wool, but in time canvas tape was used. This was dyed in different colours and interwoven to give a contrasting effect. Some chairs made at Mount Lebenon were upholstered in a form of plush called shag.

Although most chairs were finished with a finial on the back uprights, cne group are fitted with a curved bar on top of these back posts called a shawl rail, from which a cushion could be attached by tape hoops. Special types of chairs were made as low-backs, having only one or two slats, of these the loom and ironing chairs had low backs but much longer legs. The legs are braced by two box stretchers of plain turnings, and the uprights end in acorn or knob finials. Improvements in the design included a 'boot' or extra foot inserted into the back legs to support the chair when it was tilted back.

A development of the low-back chair appears in the Shaker waggon seat which was made to take two or three persons, but it is made more like a double armchair than a settee. They were used on a farm waggon in order to convert it into a carriage on social occasions.

As Brother Thomas Whitaker sums up 'The Shaker craftsmen achieved beauty through a sense of balance, conciseness, strength (though of delicate appearance) and an enduring simplicity'. Another saying of Mother Ann was 'Build as though you were to live for a thousand years, and as you would do if you knew you were to die tomorrow'.

Chapter Ten

THE AMERICAN WINDSOR CHAIR

Centred upon Philadelphia at the beginning of the eighteenth century was a new chair style based on the Windsor method of construction. This was called the Philadelphia Low-Back and it dates from about 1725. A very early reference to the Windsor chair in America appears in an inventory compiled after the death in 1708 of John Jones, a merchant of Philadelphia. Esther Singleton, writing in 1900 refers to the inventory and mentions it as listing three Windsor chairs. Bearing in mind this early date, I suspect these may well be of English make which John Jones or one of his family brought across the Atlantic to their new home when they emigrated.

Philadelphia was the main city of the State of Pennsylvania which William Penn received from Charles II in 1681 in repayment for a debt of £16,000 which was owed by the King to his father, Admiral Penn. The City's growth was due to its commerce and export trade, and even before 1685 it had been producing a considerable amount of furniture, a craft which developed until Philadelphia became the centre of Windsor chair manufacture. There is evidence of this sale of Windsor chairs in an advertisement of David Chambers dated 1748 where he mentions his Windsor chair shop on Society Hill, and a bill of 1754 records the sale of '2 Double Windsor Chairs with 6 legs' which were made by Jebediah Snowden.

There is evidence of early production of Windsor chairs in Williamsburg in Virginia, a town which has, in the past fifty years been faithfully restored to its eighteenth century glory. Here we see the combination of chairmaker with inn-keeper which was so successful in High Wycombe in the nineteenth century, for Anthony Hay who was known to have been a chairmaker in 1776, later became the proprietor of the Raleigh Tavern in Williamsburg. At Alexandria about 1798 John Hubbell also combined cabinet-making with tavern keeping. When I stayed at Williamsberg in 1965, I enjoyed both a meal at the Raleigh Tavern and a visit to the Ayscough House in which a cabinetmaker and his journeyman still carry on the craft of making fine furniture by hand. The eighteenth century tools used in the shop include frame saws, chisels, bits and braces and a

The Tavern at the American Museum in Britain, Claverton Manor, Bath, showing five different styles of Windsor chair on display.

great variety of bench, fitting and moulding planes. Still in use are the hand-powered lathes which were active when Richard Caulton of Williamsburg was announcing that he made and mended various kinds of furniture, including Windsor chairs, in the eighteenth century.

The importance of the Windsor chair in America is noticeable from the way in which it has become an accepted piece of furniture in most homes. It was made as a handsome chair in a variety of designs, one Philadelphia Quaker making no less than eight styles of Windsor chairs including some models destined for the City Hall.

The American Windsor differs considerably from the English patterns. Wallace Nutting, the American collector, was quite scathing about the latter. 'The English Windsor lacks grace, observe how stubby and shapeless the arms are, the bow is heavy without being stronger for its purpose than a lighter one. The legs are very poor features, too near the corner of the chair for strength or beauty and their turnings are very clumsy'. Although this is a very prejudiced view of an attractive traditional style, several of the differences between the chairs of these two countries are here highlighted. There were other features which help to distinguish between the two native patterns. American chairs tend to avoid the use of the cow-horn stretcher using the H-stretcher in most cases, also the decorated splat so familiar in the back of the English Windsor has never been used in the States. Possibly it was introduced after the Windsor style had gone to the Colonies and so was never properly introduced.

Despite these omissions, the Colonial craftsmen specialised in producing a very wide variety of styles, and the chairmakers have gone to great lengths to retain the popularity of the Windsor by introducing a number of specially designed writing chairs, double combed chairs, children's chairs and settees. In some instances they carried their inventive designs to border on the ridiculous.

The basic design of the early chair was based the Philadelphia Low-Back, which takes us back in period to the Queen Anne writing chairs. This well-proportioned chair appears frequently as a basic part of other patterns. It is identifiable by the leg turnings which are mostly vase or cylinder blunt arrow turned, with the legs widely splayed. The saddled seat is a wide U-shape with a straight front edge. A number of these low-backs were specially made for the Pennsylvania State Assembly House in 1778 when Francis Trumble was paid the large sum of £64.8.6d for their manufacture.

The comb-back developed quickly from the low-back, and in many chairs there is little new design work, as the seven or nine spindles were simply extended through the arm-rail and capped by a wide comb-piece with the ends sometimes shaped into curved horns or carved ears technically termed 'volute carved'. The Philadelphia comb-back is a small squat version in which the comb stands about fifteen inches above the arm bow while the New England comb-back goes to the other extreme as the spindles extend to a height of up to three feet above the arm-bow.

In later versions this arm-bow is a plain unpretentious bow instead of retaining the raised scroll of the earlier low-back pattern. The comb-back legs utilise turnings of vase and cylinder or vase and ring and the H-stretchers usually have baluster or bobbin-turned parts. One of the first claims to fame of the comb-back lies in its use by Thomas Jefferson (1743-1826) when composing the first draft of the Declaration of Independence in the late June of 1776. The suggestion has been made that the writing Windsor chair was actually designed by Jefferson. Both the draft and Jefferson's comb-back Windsor are in the collection of the American Philosophical Society of which he was President for eighteen years.

New England Fan-back armchair with braced back c.1765-1770. *(H. F. Du Pont Winterthur Museum)*

Although the bow-back or sackback as it was called in America, was popular c.1750-1820, it did not sweep across the market in the same way it did in England, overshadowing and often replacing other styles. Perhaps the lack of the ornamental splat made it too plain a chair for Colonial taste. The arm-bow is often supported higher above the seat than its English counterpart, and the bow itself takes on an almost balloon shape. In order to overcome its plainness or to add to its comfort, a variety of abbreviated combs were added in some chairs above the bow acting as head rests, this is a feature not encountered in English designs.

The first session of the Continental Congress met at the Carpenter's Hall, Philadelphia in 1775, and the members used the Windsor chairs with which it had been hurredly furnished. A year later, a proper meeting of the Congress took place at the Assembly Chamber of the Independence Hall, and at that time the chairs in use were bow-backs. A number of these had been ordered in October 1775. 'Ordered, that one dozen and a half of Windsor chairs be immediately procured for the Use of the House'. These were again made by Francis Trumble and paid for May 31st 1776.

Unfortunately the Independence Hall was seized by the British Occupation forces in 1777-1778 and was used as a hospital and prison. Few of the furnishings survived, so when the Continental Congress moved back to Philadelphia, new furniture was required and almost one hundred and fifty Windsor chairs, round-back, low-back and sack-back were made, also by Francis Trumble.

Robert Edge Pine, an English painter who migrated to the United States in 1784, commenced a painting 'Congress Voting Independence' which shows the Assembly Chamber in which this voting took place. He knew most of the Signers and his portraits of each formed the main interest of the massive painting. Of particular interest is the figure of Benjamin Franklin (1706-1790) in the centre foreground which is clearly seated on a bow-back Windsor chair. Pine did not finish the painting, for he died of apoplexy in 1788, so it was completed by Edward Savage.

The next stage in development was the fan-back, and this generally has vase and ring turnings in the legs and in the two outer turned spindles supporting the back. The fan-back which was popular as a side chair, was made c.1750-1800 and was probably the first Windsor chair made specially as a lady's chair in a smaller size. A most attractive example of the fan-back is in the Museum of Fine Arts in Boston, which originally belonged to Tutor Henry Flint of Harvard University where he taught for the extraordinary long period of 1699-1760. In his will of 1758 he bequeathed his 'easy green chair' to his niece and later it passed to the writer Dr. Oliver Wendall Holmes (1809-1894).

The loop-back Windsor is an alternative name for a similar chair to the English single bow-back in which the bow is U-shaped and enters the seat on each side with the arm-pieces jointed to the bow. The American chairs are often more narrowly waisted than the English version, although modern single bow chairs in this country are being designed with this feature. The loop-back must be the style of chair referred to as 'oval back' which George Washington (1732-1799) bought in 1796 from Gilbert and Robert Gaw of Philadelphia, these were made with the new style 'bamboo' turnings which were used extensively in America. The label on the seat of the chairs bears the slogan 'orders from the West Indies or any part of the Continent will be punctually attended to'. Washington bought twenty-seven chairs for forty-eight dollars! which shows how inexpensive they were in those days. These chairs were used on the portico at Mount Vernon. The legs of the loop-back have bobbin or vase turnings in the legs with a bobbin turned H-stretcher; they are generally dated 1750-1800 and are sometimes called balloon chairs.

George Washington did not always remain loyal to American furniture as E. T. Joy points out in a letter written by Washington to his London agent in 1755 'send me one dozen strong chairs of about 15 shillings apiece . . . I have one dozen chair that were made in this country; neat but too weak for common sitting'. When the Wiltshire clothier Henry Wansey returned from a visit to the States in 1796 he advised prospective emigrants to take 'plenty of kitchen furniture, feather beds and mattresses. All these articles are dear and bad if had in America'.

The arch-back Windsor is a style in which the back bow, instead of being jointed into a separate arm bow, is actually extended and the ends shaped to form the arms. To produce this elaborate shape much skill is necessary as the wood is steamed and clamped into a special frame until dry. Archbacks appear to have been made primarily in New England. Thomas H. Ormsbee feels they 'represent a high point in the craft'.

Like the arch-back, the rod-back has no identical English counterpart, although the squareness of the shape is very reminiscent of the Mendlesham chair. It has a flat straight back rail or comb into which the spindles, often with bamboo turnings, are socketed. The arms flair outwards from the back supports and they are supported by bamboo ringed uprights. The legs also have this simple bamboo decoration and show considerably less outward splay than is normal in American Windsor chairs. Many of these rod-backs were painted black and ornamented with

New England Bow-back armchair with comb. *(American Museum in Britain)*

decoration of Shereton design. These rod-back chairs show a distinctive break away from the traditional designs, and as they were made c.1800-1830, may well have been influenced by the Shereton pattern books. They also incorporate the box stretcher in the underframe.

This chair was developed further and we find the arrow back is the next stage c.1810-1835. This retains many of the features of the rod-back, but in place of the bamboo turned rod, a broad arrow-shaped spindle is introduced. The back of the chair is invariably made with a strong backward sweep and the top rail is not necessarily straight but often shaped. The legs and stretcher, which are again of the box type are bamboo ringed, and the legs have little splay. The arms are shaped in a cyma-curve and have rolled ends, this chair was made in quantities as a rocking chair, often painted in Shereton design.

It seems probable that the Philadelphia chairmaker did not manufacture Windsor side or single chairs until after 1770 and one manufacturer supplied twelve Windsor chairs 'without arms' in 1779. The ingenuity of these chairmakers is exhibited in the writing Windsor chairs they produced. There were several problems in making these, as the chair, if it was to have strong supports for the writing arm, could not be designed symmetrically. Sometimes the arm was fixed, and then the arm supports might be fixed to a bobtail piece which formed part of the seat itself. Other times it was a swivel writing surface which was attached to a heavy strut replacing the normal arm support. Occasionally a drawer was fitted under the writing arm, and a second drawer might also be arranged to slop underneath the seat. The Windsor chair styles used for the writing chairs were chiefly low-back, bow-back, rod-backs, comb-backs and even firehouse chairs. Perhaps the most unusual ones to survive include an arch-back rocking writing chair . . . surely the height of luxury, while a rather rare left-handed rod-back writing Windsor chair dated c.1825, painted red, can be found in the Henry Ford Museum.

Other furniture based on the Windsor style of construction includes the wide range of settees which, like the writing chair, were made in as many styles as possible. They could be up to seven feet in length and the comb-back version might have a wooden comb across the back almost five feet in length supported by a long row of spindles. The other main design was the bow-back and this with its series of three interlaced bow gave a rather elegant effect, with a smaller version of about four feet wide being produced as 'love-seats'.

Most unusual is the sole survivor of a range of Windsor riding chairs, this example once owned by Lord Fairfax c.1781. Thomas, sixth Baron

Fairfax, came to Virginia to live on his American estates after being jilted, and finally settled there, making acquaintance with the young George Washington. When Washington was only sixteen, Fairfax entrusted to him the task of surveying his property at Shenandoah. Both Lord Fairfax and George Washington had one of these Windsor riding chairs, and the latter bought another for his mother in 1774 which cost £40. The two-wheeled riding chair was similar to the later buggy and the example at Mount Vernon consists of the rod-back side chair mounted on a platform which rests on the shafts between two large coach wheels.

As in England, one of the more popular chairs for office use was the low-back of which the Philadelphia low-back was the eighteenth century pattern. This was revived in the 1830's as the smoker's bow, a chair described more fully in chapter eight. Variations in America included the Firehouse Windsor c.1850-70 which was used widely in furnishing the quarters of the American volunteer fire companies. They were also popular in hotels and business offices. The difference between it and the smoker's bow are slight. The bow-scroll is less decorative and usually pierced with a hand grip, whilst the arms end in a simple knuckle and the underframe is a single box stretcher.

The Captain's chair c.1875-1900 takes its name from its use in the pilot houses of the boats steaming up and down the Mississippi. Again its difference from the smoker's bow is slight, just the use of a double box stretcher instead of the H-stretcher, and the arms continue in a curve downwards and are socketed into the seat. These were factory made in large quantities, up to the 1900's and were used in court houses, school rooms and offices.

Most Windsors of the 18th century were painted and the range of colours included yellow, black, white and green. In 1795 Walter MacBridge advertised his Windsor chairs in finishes which were 'Japanned in any colour and neatly flowered'. There has been a feeling that Windsor chairs were not originally upholstered, and indeed the early antique Windsor which was upholstered was at one time considered to have lost some of its value. So it is a body-blow to this theory when labels which can be dated as 1797 carry the legend 'William W. Galation . . . Upholsterer and paper-hanger' are still adhered to the underside of chairs. Only a little later Windsors were advertised as 'stuffed in seat and brass nails'. When the chairmaking firm of Gomme in High Wycombe commenced work in the nineteenth century, their first model was a Windsor Goldsmith chair which was upholstered and finished with brass nails!

The woods used in America for their Windsor chair were pine, or whitewood for the seats, ash or hickory for the spindles, the turned legs were made of maple, yellow birch or beech, the hoops or bows used ash, oak or beech.

Foremost among the painted Windsor type furniture was the work of the Pennsylvania Dutch who came from the German Palatine. They arrived in the State about 1673, before William Penn had established his claim on the territory. They kept to their national crafts and their characteristics long after handmade furniture had ceased to be made on a craft basis, and the feature of their furniture was the practice of painting it in strong colours.

The Pennsylvania Dutch painted settee is of Windsor construction and has a wide top rail supported by four canted and turned uprights. A lower rail is linked to the seat by some twelve to fifteen turned spindles. It has a solid wooden seat with the legs braced by a series of single box stretchers, the main background colour was often brown or black. This settee was chiefly manufactured c.1820-1850.

The Windsor construction is also apparent in the Hitchcock settee cradle, an ingenious rocking settee with a wide top rail supported by twelve slender spindles which enter the seat. The noticeable feature is the supporting fence or rail which slots into two holes in the seat enabling a cradle to be made which allows the baby and mother to gently rock together. As with many other types of chair, the rockers was produced in almost every style of Windsor construction, but the wide comb and stick construction used in the Boston rocker was the favourite. It was made with a solid wooden seat rolled over at the front and sharply curved upwards at the back to fit the figure. Seven or nine plain spindles supported the top rail and the whole chair is painted or grained. Gold, stencilled or painted decorations are usually to be found on the front of the seat and the comb. One writer recalls a housekeeper, when asked what she had done during the day replied 'Sometimes I rock an' read, or I rock an' knit, an' then again sometime I just set an' rock'!

Chapter Eleven

THE HANDMADE REVIVAL

There is a tale concerning William Morris (1834-96) which recounts how, while still in his teens, he refused to visit the 1851 Great Exhibition because everything there was 'wonderfully ugly'. Whether this is true is uncertain, but what cannot be denied is the important part played by Morris, and his great influence upon all aspects of Victorian art, decoration and furniture, in the latter half of the century.

Whilst capable of turning his hand expertly to most crafts, his artistic ideas spread much wider than his immediate circle. His hatred of the contemporary industrial system and the increasing use of machinery caused him to advocate a society in which the arts should be created 'by the people, for the people as a joy to the maker and user'. Like Morris, William Blake felt strongly about this problem, writing in his famous verse 'Jerusalem':

> . . . And was Jerusalem builded here
> Among these dark Satanic Mills?
> I will not cease from mental fight,
> Nor shall my sword sleep in my hand
> Till we have built Jerusalem
> In England's green and pleasant land.

To put his ideas into practice, William Morris founded a firm in 1861, later to be called Morris & Co., which was formed through the co-operation of several artistic friends. The output of this firm in the field of furniture was channelled into two categories, one Morris termed State furniture in which he re-created the medieval masterpieces of the past in vivid colours and harmonious shapes. This was very close to the heart of William Morris who was not an innovator or modernist, instead he looked back to the age of Chaucer and Mallory from which he drew his inspiration. The other class of furniture, and to us the more important was called 'workaday' in which the design of the village craftsmen were re-vitalised and made 'simple to the last degree', resulting in the production of a chair called the 'Sussex' chair in c.1865 and other rural

The Sussex Chair, a turned wood spindle chair, painted and with a rush seat, made by Morris & Co. c.1870-80. *(Victoria and Albert Museum)*

furniture. The twin concept covering these two categories was summed up in his statement 'have nothing in your home that you do not know to be useful or believe to be beautiful'.

The Sussex chair indicates how he has taken a factory item which was losing its identity as a rural style, and re-designed it with a simplicity of line and an effortless use of ornament which does not over-awe the materials with which it is made. The arms, which are canted in an outward sweep from the back stays, are socketed through the seat into the upper stretcher for firmness, while the use of a slender undecorated box stretcher and back and arm stays, give a slenderness to the design yet do not reduce its strength.

Joan Gloag recalls with glee the appreciation of William Morris which appeared in the 'Cabinet Maker and Art Furnisher' after his death in 1896, for it confirmed that he 'blessed and made popular the old Wycombe rush-bottomed chair' and another note in the same year blazoned the fact that the Windsor chair had earlier 'been sent below stairs because they smelt of the kitchen. Now, thanks to common sense, they are 'coming up' again, and it is our pleasure to do what we can to encourage them'.

Others connected with the firm included the chief furniture designer Philwp Webb and the artists Edward Burne-Jones (1833-98), William Holman Hunt (1827-1910) and Gabriel Dante Rossetti (1828-1882). John Betjeman, surprisingly enough, also appreciates the work of Morris 'who swept away the needless knick-knacks, opened the window and let the fresh garden suburb air in and freed us from slavery to the machine'. But although William Morris made much outward protests against this use of machinery, his firm utilised the products of firms which used it extensively. And according to Edward Joy it was Morris's 'general denunciation of the evils of machinery (which) helped to postpone serious consideration of machine-made furniture'.

The output of Morris & Co. continued long after the death of Morris in 1896 and the firm only ceased production in 1940. Inevitably the concept changed but the spirit of the earlier tradition was faithfully continued by the Cotswold School which was centred around the artist-craftsman Ernest Gimson (1864-1919). Gimson had met William Morris in 1884 when he had stayed at the Gimson house while lecturing at Leicester. Impressed by young Ernest's drawing, he gave him a letter of introduction to the firm of J. D. Sedding, architects, in London. Here he met two fellow trainees Ernest and Sidney Barnsley who were to figure largely in his future plans. In time Ernest Gimson decided to direct his interest to furniture and with the Barnsleys and another architect formed the firm of

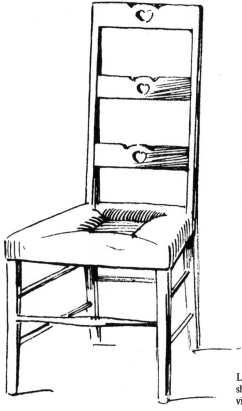

Ladderback in the style of Vosey with heart shape holes in the slats, upholstered with a vicarage seat. c.1905.

Kenton & Co. which lasted two years, after which Ernest Gimson and the Barnsley brothers moved out to the Cotswolds where they felt the industrial age could not reach them and where the traditional village crafts still flourished.

Gimson wrote in 1890 'I have been spending my time in unsuccessful hunts after country cottages' and after one or two tries, settled at Sopperton near Pinsbury in 1903. Some years earlier Gimson had spent a fortnight with the Herts chairmaker Philip Closset and, I quote, 'learned the secrets of chairmaking' returning with a pole-lathe. But whilst he was an excellent designer one of his men stated that he was not very good at chair-making.

The first chairs were based on the Morris designs of the 'Sussex' chair and on the ladderbacks he had seen made in Hertfordshire, but soon an individuality began to show through. Just as Morris is remembered for his spindle-back, so Gimson's ladderbacks breathe the spirit of his design. They are usually rush-seated and have elegant and slender turned legs, stays and stretchers, while the design of the back slats allows them to increase in broadness as they proceed up the chair, producing a beautifully proportioned and balanced design. One of his craftsmen, Edward Gardiner recalls 'He had a number of chairs made at High Wycombe to his drawing of what I call the Gimson chair. He made the chair himself when at Pinbury Park and he did not like the factory chairs . . . the only good thing about them were the rush seats, they were very good!' Fortunately for Wm. Birch of High Wycombe, they were more successful with Gimson's jointed chair which they produced with an Art Nouveau influence in 1900.

The group produced a wide range of furniture, selecting the timber most suitable for a particular piece of work, and utilising techniques which lightened the appearance of the finished chair. The work of the Barnsley Brothers should not be overlooked, although they tend to be overshadowed by Gimson in the evaluation of the Cotswold School. The group was joined by Peter Waals, the Dutch cabinet-maker, in 1901, who, after the death of Gimson decided to establish new workshops with some other craftsmen at Chalford in Gloucestershire. The effect of this team is summed up by Sir George Trevelyan 'To the end he maintained unswervingly the absolute standard of woodwork on which the Cotswold Tradition had grown up, and the pride of great craftsmanship which held together his team'. The aims of the Cotswold School are evaluated by A. E. Bradshaw. 'There is no evidence that Gimson and his associates sought to influence the design of work sold in the shops, or that they propagated any social theories; they were not writers, but craftsmen and artists, and the only records they have left are in their work'.

L'Art Nouveau was the rage for a short period which followed and it rapidly affected many aspects of decoration and furniture, yet art historians agree this influence was concentrated much more effectively on the Continent than in England. The Cotswold School ignored it, and the intricacies of its designs, while they may have lingered in the 1920's, are seldom nowadays revived in their full splendour. Mr. Allan Janes of High Wycombe was quite scathing about its effect on furniture design, for according to him it meant 'taking quite a good design, reversing all the nice lines, for instance, turning the baluster of a nice Queen Anne chair, bottom upwards, and piercing it with holes to represent such things as lilies, pomegranates and Prince of Wales feathers. It is hard to say which

Cotswold School spindle chair in yew, bobbin turned, with rush seat. Designed by Ernest Gimson and made at the Daneway House workshops, Sapperton. c.1905. *(Victoria and Albert Museum)*

was the greatest abomination that or the so-called 'modern' furniture that became the fashion after the First World War'. An equally damning comment comes from Joseph Thorp, the 'sad progeny of the art nouveau, with its meandering tulips and inconsequent squiggles and dots, extravagant, impractical, of an intense unrestfulness'.

Yet for Wm. Birch of High Wycombe, it extended their export trade considerably and the firm produced numerous designs for Liberty's and for Continental appetites which reflect the stark lines and uncompromising shapes of the period. Curves are not important and it is the verticals which play the more important part. The back stays frequently rise high above the back rail with artificial shapes imposed at head level to carry the eye to the full height. Another feature was the practice of dropping the stretchers of the chairs and tables almost to floor level. In some designs, such as the chair designed by E. G. Pannett, this was acceptable, but in other slimmer chairs this form of stretcher could produce a chair that was structurally less than sound. A designer of importance connected with Art Nouveau was C. F. A. Vosey (1857-1941) whose designs owed nothing to the past. He is regarded as 'par excellence the prophet of that school of artistic expression which finds its outlet in a revolt against the accepted conventions'. His importance lies in the fact that he also realised the necessity to design for mechanical production.

The rural chairs were not forgotten in this decorative style of the early twentieth century, and Wm. Birch's design and cost books contain examples of their designers' ingenuity. The ladderback appears quite frequently, one with the heart-shaped holes associated with Vosey, upholstered and bearing the title of 'Vicarage' seat. Another ladderback has slats simply designed with the stays extended well above the top rail. The Windsor also appears, this time as a smoker's bow with an upholstered panel mounted above the arm-rail. Whilst in another design which carries the stamp of E. G. Pannett, the concept of the smoker's bow is translated into an Art Nouveau oak chair with considerable skill.

This concept of chairmaking where designers plan chairs with the machine-production specifically in mind carries us into the age of the modern Colleges of Design, and the importance of the new ideas emerging from them.

Writing in 1937 Pevsner reported that 'not more than twenty real designers are employed in Wycombe. Most of the Manufacturers cannot afford a designer'. This was a fairly common state throughout the furniture trade, but several figures appeared to fill the vacuum. Sir Ambrose Heal (1872-1959) who worked on the design policy of the

Tottenham Court Road firm of Heal & Son, re-introduced the standards of 'well chosen material, admirable proportion, harmonious design and rigid economy of ornament'. In 1918 he produced 'A plan for simplicity in cottage furniture' with an illustrated catalogue including much rural chairs, including Windsors, Gimson style ladderbacks, the Sussex chair and a certain amount of Jacobean reproduction furniture. He deplored the fact that 'in the cottage of the gentility ... we find all the pretentious fussiness of the suburban villa, the absurd antimacassars ... It may be objected that our designs err on the side of excessive plainness. Our answer is that economy has been studied everywhere except at the expense of sound construction'.

The next range of designers include several whose contacts with the Cotswold School give a link to their flair and design simplicity. Peter Waals (1870-1937) became design adviser to Loughborough Training College, and after his death Edward Barnsley, son of Sidney Barnsley, continued the tradition of handmade furniture and also took the post of design adviser at Loughborough. This generation of designers and hand craftsmen became linked with the new colleges which were beginning to play an important part in the apprenticeship schemes, and in training the newcomers to the furniture world. In Wycombe the trend started in 1893 when the first properly equipped technical school commenced giving day and evening classes in art, in furniture making and in carving. As the town and the industry progressed, so did the school, until in 1957 the new Technical College was opened. Here were trained such designers as Robin Day who won 1st prize in a furniture design competition organised by the Museum of Modern Art in New York, or J. H. Easen whose designs and carvings are to be seen in the mace presented by the House of Commons to the new Governments of Rhodesia and Nyasaland. While the work of students at Loughborough Training College, Shoreditch Training College and other such centres in England, exhibit the originality and ability of the younger students and designers.

John Harrison truly commented 'it is neither true nor relevant to say that hand-made furniture is better than machine-made furniture. They both have their individual and quite distinctive qualities, and, of course, there are good and bad examples of each type. Machine-made furniture has become an essential part of this industrial nation ... (but) hand craftsmanship has an important part to play in the foreseeable future.

Examples of fine machine-made chair, are to be seen and enjoyed as the manufacturers have reacted to the post-war interest in the fabrics, silverware, pottery and furniture in the past. A faithful copy is no longer the easy way out. New designs should give us more than this, so while some of the large manufacturers can turn back to the eighteenth century design books, and Lucian Ercolani with his principle 'the basis of design is fitness of purpose' can recreate the spirit of the traditional Windsor chair, the ladderback or the old Colonial chair. Other firms with much ado and publicity are supplying first class furniture of high standard.

A whole range of pine furniture incorporating the ladderback is produced under the title 'Ducal Country Style' where 'the colour of sunrise in its carefree youth, pine mellows gracefully with age into the deeper tones of a golden sunset'. But however sentimental the approach, the rush-seated chairs have a firmness and simplicity it is a pleasure to handle. In the catalogue drawers of the Design Centre, prominent are the chairs of the firm of Neville Neal of Stockton, whose spindle-back rocker is designed by Ernest Gimson, and their range of ladderbacks boast the use of coppice ash poles.

In the Windsor range, Batheaston Chairmakers report themselves as specialists in Windsor chairs with each chair individually made by craftsmen. Sturdy in design, made of traditional elm and yew wood, the rich grain shows through the present a rural chair with Gothic, Chippendale or wheelback splats which is how this style has survived so long.

When Frank Hudson, master carver of West Wycombe was talking about the future of the trade, it was encouraging to find that the Technical College could still supply him with sufficient interested youngsters to allow his workshop to carry three apprentices in this demanding craft. There is hope in the chair trade when these young apprentices can still experience what Frank Hudson terms 'the excited interest you always get if you are in craft trade'.

As for the chair itself, we have seen its design change radically over the years to a state where one hesitates to consider what will happen next. So I will go along with the philosophy of Joseph Rykavert 'Not that chairs are bound to be immutable. I dare say that they will change even more rapidly in the future. There are indeed cultures where sitting cross-legged on the floor or simply squatting are regarded as perfectly adequate postures of repose, and we may for many other reasons turn to the example of certain Central Australian or South African Bushman tribes as a model of the good society on which to refashion our cultural institutions. But until that movement takes effect, or we devise a wholly new framework which may demand an analogous posture, we will continue to sit on chairs'.

GLOSSARY

Adze — a curved dished form of axe used to cut away the surplus wood in saddling the wooden seat of a Windsor chair.

Arch-back Windsor — an American Windsor chair where the arms and the high arched back are made of one length of timber steamed and bent in a frame.

Arrow-back Windsor — an American Windsor chair style with the sticks replaced by arrow-topped rods and the back of the chairs sweeps backward.

Astley-Cooper chair — a child's straight-backed chair designed to correct stooping, c.1820.

Back chair or Back stool — the first development of the side chair, early 17th century when the back was fitted to the oak joined stool. Three styles, the Yorkshire, Derbyshire and Lancashire were popular.

Balloon back chair — a type of light elegant cane-seated chair where the back has an open frame, a large number were made in Wycombe c.1840-1900.

Balloon back Windsor chair — an 18th century variant in which the back comb is so small that the sticks bow inwards into a curved shape to fit into it.

Ball and steeple finial — ball with a series of rings diminishing in size which surmounts a back stay.

Baluster Leg — the name given to the normal turned leg as made by the bodgers, also to any spindle turnings, especially those with a vase shape.

Bamboo ringing — a form of turning used on some American Windsors to simulate bamboo sticks.

Beetle — a barrel-shaped mallet, banded each end with metal rings, used with a splitting-out-hatchet or wedge in splitting logs into quarters.

Bender chair — an early 19th century spindle arm-chair similar to the later Sussex chair.

Bentwood chair — a type of chair made c.1850 by Michael Thonet in Vienna. Lengths of timber are steamed and bent into shape, from this all parts of the chair with the exception of the seat are formed.

Berger Bow or Bergere — a development of the smoker's bow in which the armbow sweeps upwards into a high bow. The spindles are generally replaced by splats.

Billet — the roughly shaped chair leg before it is turned on the pole-lathe.

Bobbin-frame chair — a chair of turned pieces, c.16th century.

Bobtail — the small extension at the back of the seat of a Windsor chair into which the bracing stays are socketed.

Bow — the curved section used as a back bow or arm bow. Made of Yew or any other supple wood which can be steamed and bent around a frame.

Bow-back chair — a Windsor chair in which the back sticks are contained within a curved back bow.

Box — the lower handle of a pit saw.

Box stretcher — a stretcher in which the supports join the chair legs in a box shape and do not cross the underframe.

Bow-saw — a saw used for cutting curved shapes, with a narrow blade which is kept taut with a twisted string tightening the framework.

Brace — a cranked tool with a chuck for gripping boring bits.

Bracing sticks — the support which extends from the comb or bow to the bob-tail and give added support to the back.

Breast bib — a hardwood bib worn across the chest of a workman into which the head of a brace fits when drilling holes for leg-joints, etc.

Brewster chair — American turned spindle chair c.1650-1700 which has two rows of spindles in the back, takes its name from William Brewster, one of the Pilgrim Fathers.

Buckle-back chairs — a nineteenth century dining room chair in which an additional decoration in the yoke gives the effect of a buckle.

Cabriole Leg — an elaborate leg form introduced c.1700 and used on Windsor chairs from c.1740.

Cardiganshire chair — a three-legged low-back chair in Windsor style eighteenth century.

Carver — a term introduced in the nineteenth century to distinguish between the armchair used at the head of the dining table and the small elbow chair found elsewhere in the house.

Carver Chair — American turned spindle chair c.1650-1700, which has one row of spindles in the back, it takes its name from John Carver, Governor of Plymouth 1620-21.

Chippendale Windsor — a style in which the splat is carved in imitation of the ribbon pattern used on the splat of a Chippendale chair c.1770-1850.

Comb — the straight top rail of an eighteenth century Windsor chair into which the sticks are socketed, also called the cresting rail.

Comb-back chair – a form of Windsor chair in which the sticks are socketed into a straight comb instead of a bow.

Cow-horn stretcher – a form of stretcher where the front legs of the chair are braced by a curved bow from which two spurs link the bow to the back legs, hence the alternative name spur stretcher. Also called Crinoline stretcher.

Cresting-rail – another name for a comb, but also used for the top back rail of other chairs.

Crinoline Stretcher – alternative name for Cow-horn stretcher.

Dancing Jenny – see Frame saw.

Deck chair – a form of folding chair which originated in the Glastonbury chair, became the Derby chair and finally was called the Steamer chair before being called the more modern name.

Derby chair – the name used for the steamer or deck chair c.1850-1890.

Derbyshire back chair – an oak chair c.1660 which has two straight horizontal rails, the lower part of the upper rail arcaded and joined to the lower rail by two turned spindles with bobbin finials decorating both rails.

Digestive chair – a nineteenth century name for the rocking chair.

Dogs – the iron spikes used to secure timbers to the saw-pit framework when being sawn, also the wooden long legged saw-horse used when sawing the trunk into logs.

Double-H stretcher – a form of stretcher with two cross members linking the side stretchers instead of the one cross-rail in the H-stretcher.

Drawknife – a sharp knife with a handle at each end which allows it to be pulled towards the workman, used to clear excess wood quickly, also called the draw-shave.

Drunkard's chair – a wide spindle chair of late eighteenth century that is wide enough to take two persons, sometimes called a Derby and Joan chair.

Ears – the curved ends of the Windsor comb.

Elbow chair – a small armchair often a lady's chair.

Fan-back chair – one in which the comb is wider than the seat, causing the sticks to fan outwards.

Farthingale chair – a high upholstered chair with no arms, late sixteenth and seventeenth century, probably used with a footstool.

Fiddle-back – an unpierced splay in violin outline, used with early comb-back chairs.

Finial – decorative ornament at the top of the back stays or uprights of a chair.

Frame-saw — widely used in chair-making, also called the Up-and-down-saw; Dancing Betty; Jesus Christ Saw. The blade is usually set in the centre of a wooden frame, and it is used in an up and down motion.

Froe — a metal wedge-like blade with a handle at right angles used with a beetle in splitting small logs.

Garden machine — an eighteenth century wheel chair.

Glastonbury chair — a folding X-chair c sixteenth century which developed into the nineteenth century folding chair.

Gossip chair — a term used for a single or side chair, originally seventeenth century, later used in the nineteenth century.

Gothic — the name given to the romantic pseudo-gothic styles of the 1750's which gradually modified to reappear in Regency styles. It was again revived in the mid-Victorian period.

Gothic Windsor — a Windsor chair c.1760-80 in which the sticks are replaced by large open-work window splats in a Gothic manner, sometimes the round bow is shaped as a pointed arch.

H-Stretcher — the most common form of stretcher in which the two side pieces which join the front and back legs, are linked across the middle of the underframe by a third straight stretcher.

Holdfast — a form of cramp for holding the job on to the bench while being worked upon.

Hoof foot — a form of cabriole leg in which the foot appears as a goat's hoof c.1700 onwards.

Horns — the ears at the ends of the comb-piece, when they have been extended and curved upwards — most noticeable in American chairs.

Joyned chairs or stools — an Elizabethan stool or chair made of heavy oak rails secured at the joints by wooden pegs.

Jump-ups — a type of children's high chair in which the seat is fixed with a thumbscrew on top of a small table or stand.

Kerf — a groove made by a single saw-cut.

Ladder-back — the style in which the back stays of the chair are linked by a series of back rails or yokes giving the effect of a ladder.

Lancashire Back chair — the name given to one of the styles of back-chairs c.1600.

Lancashire ladderback — popular chair in c.1750 which had five or six serpentine splats.

Lancashire Windsor — a heavy turned Windsor chair with the back bow inserted over the armbow which is often supported by spindles instead of sticks. Also called a Yorkshire Windsor.

Lath and Baluster chair — a Wycombe made lath back chair into which a pierced splat or baluster has been introduced.

Lath back chair — a type of comb-back chair made in Wycombe c.1850-90 in which the sticks have been replaced by shaped laths.

Legging-up — the assembly of the seat and lower parts of the chair.

Loop-back — an American type of Windsor chair which is similar to the English single bow, but which is more waisted near the seat.

Mendlesham chair — a regional Windsor chair made in Suffolk early nineteenth century with straight back rail.

Morris chair — *see* Sussex chair.

Pit-saw — a large two handled saw with two detachable handles. It tapers in width from about seven inches at the top to three or four inches at the base.

Poppets — the lathe headstock; especially the loose head and tail stock used with the pole-lathe.

Puritan slat-back — American ladder-back chair 1670-1770 with rush seat and three wide concave slats in the back.

Rod-back chair — an American Windsor which has a straight rail similar to an English Mendlesham chair, and the sticks often have bamboo ringings, and a box-stretcher is used. c.1800-1830.

Roman Spindle chair — a Windsor chair with a heavy comb in which the spindles have been decorated with turned swells and rings c.1870-90.

Sack-back — an American name for the bow-back.

Saddle Seat or saddling — a seat shaped with a depression each side of a low ridge towards the front, adzed out of the timber to make the solid wooden seat comfortable.

Sausage turning — a turning used often in double-H stretchers that resembles a length of short plump sausages.

Scole chair — a type of Windsor regional chair, made at Scole in Norfolk, which appear to be so similar to the Mendlesham chair to be linked with it.

Scroll-back chairs — a popular Windsor chair c.1830 in which the tops of the back-stays are turned or scrolled over.

Serpentine X-stretcher — an X-crossed stretcher with curved members instead of straight ones.

Shaw-rail — the top rail across the top of the Shaker slat-back from which a cushion can be attached.

Side chair — a chair without arms, also called a single chair or a gossip chair.

Sills and strakes — the two sets of timbers which form the platform of the sawpit on which the tree trunk is positioned for sawing.

Single chair — a chair without arms, also called a side chair or gossip chair.

Slat back chair — the American name for a ladderback chair.

Smoker's bow — a low-back Windsor chair made in Great Britain and America in which the armbow is also the backbow and is surmounted by a heavy scroll c.1830-1930.

Spindle back — a forerunner of the lath back c.1850-80, having a heavy comb supported by plain turned spindles which swell slightly to fit the small of the back.

Spindle chair — a type of chair with turned spindles or balusters in rows in the back.

Splats or balusters — the decorated pierced upright in the centre of the back in an English Windsor chair, also called banister.

Spokeshaves — a small two-handled planing tool which is used in shaping bows and cleaning off seats, etc. Includes variations such as the devil, a scraper with a vertical blade; a travisher, with a curved blade and a cleaning off iron which smooths the seat surface after the shaves have done their work.

Spoon drills — a drill bit which is spoon-shaped which was used in chair-making as it cuts cleanly and will start at any angle.

Spur-stretcher — alternative name for cow-horn stretcher.

Stays — the back outside uprights of a chair which support the comb or cresting rail.

Steamer chair — a folding chair with four or six legs, formerly called the Derby chair, which was used on the steamers crossing the Atlantic, and so was given this name.

Stick-back — any chair of Windsor construction which uses plain sticks in the back, usually used for Windsor chairs without splats.

Stretcher — the turned pieces underneath the seat which brace the legs and make them firm.

Sussex chair — a rural spindle chair re-designed and produced by Morris & Co. c.1865.

Thrown chair — a chair made of turned pieces made on a lathe also called bobbin-frame chairs, from sixteenth century.

Tiller — the long T-shaped upper handle of the pit-saw which guides the saw in the saw-kerf.

Thonet chair — *see* Bentwood chair.

Up-and-down-saw — alternative name for the Frame saw.

Vase and cylinder turning — a form of turning which incorporates a vase and cylinder in the design.

Vase and ring turning — a turning using the vase and ring shapes.

Wedge — a wide metal wedge or an axe which is used with the beetle to split the logs into quarters.

Wheelback Windsor — a low-back chair in which the splat has been pierced with the wheel motif.

Windsor splats — large openwork splats found chiefly in the Gothic Windsors c.1760-80.

X-stretcher — a stretcher in which the legs are braced by an underframe which joins the legs diagonally being jointed in the centre, form a cross shape.

Yoke or yoke-rails — the horizontal decorated rail in the middle of the back of a nineteenth century chair.

Yorkshire back chair — this oak joyned chair c.1660 has two arched horizontal rails with finials suspended below the rails.

Yorkshire spindle back — eighteenth century side chair with two or three rows of spindles in the back.

Yorkshire Windsor chair — this is an alternative name for the heavier chair also called Lancashire Windsors.

BIBLIOGRAPHY

Agius, Pauline. 101 chairs. 1968.

Arnold, J. Shell book of country crafts. 1960.

Aslin, Elizabeth. 19th Century English Furniture. 1962.

Bale, M. Powis. Woodworking machinery, its rise, progress and construction. 1880. 3rd ed. 1914.

Ballad – The lamentable fall of Queen Eleanor *in* The Roxburghe Ballads. Ballad Society. 1874.

Barnes, Mr. *tape* (High Wycombe P.L.)

Beer, G. L. The origins of the British Colonial System 1578-1660. 1933.

Betjeman, John. We beg to differ: – comments in 'Furniture design set free' by David Joel. 1969.

Blamey, Montague. *tape* (High Wycombe P.L)

Bradshaw, A. E. Handmade furniture in the 20th Century. 1962.

Burrough, B. G. Ernest Gimson. Connoisseur. 1969, pp. 228-32; 8-14.

Burrows, David. Ernest Gimson 1864-1919. 1969.

Bury, Adrian. Mr. Goodchild's immortal chairs, Everybody. 2nd October 1948 pp. 14-15.

Case of the Cane-chair makers humbly present to the consideration of the Honourable the Commons in Parliament Assembled. 1680.

Census of Woodlands 1947-49. Forestry Commission.

Dean, George R. (letter dated 25th October 1955). High Wycombe P.L.

Defoe, Daniel. Tour through the whole Island of Great Britain. 1724-7.

Eland, G. The Chilterns and the Vale. 1911.

Ercolani, Lucian. Furniture still has a placemong the fine Arts. Cabinet Maker. Jan. 19th 1973, i-iv.

Gaines, Edith. The rocking chair in America. Antiques, Feb. 1971 pp. 238-40.

Gardiner, Edward *in* Burrows, David 'Ernest Gimson' 1969.

Gloag, John. The Englishman's chair. 1964.

Gloag, John. The nomenclature of mid-Victorian chairs. Connoisseur, Aug. 1968 pp. 233-6.

Gloag, John. The rocking chair in Victorian England. Antiques, Feb. 1971 pp. 241-4.

Goodman, W. L. The history of woodworking tools. 1964 rp. 1971.

Goyne, Nancy A. American Windsor Chairs. Antiques 1969 pp. 538-43.

Haines, W. O. *tape* (High Wycombe P.L.)

Harman, Edward. *tape* (High Wycombe P.L.)

Hawkins, C. F. More work for our town. N.A.F.T.A. News Dec. 1938.

Heal, Ambrose. London Furniture makers 1660-1840. 1953.

Heal's Catalogues 1853-1934: Middle class furnishing. 1972.

Hogg, Garry. Country crafts and craftsmen. 1959.

Hopkins, Harry. England is rich. 1957.

Hopkinson, James. Memoirs of a Victorian Cabinet maker. 1968.

Hudson, Frank. *tape* (High Wycombe P.L.)

Hughes, T. Cottage antiques. 1967.

Hughes, Therle. Pocket book of furniture. 1960.

Hursthouse, Charles. New Zealand. 1861.

Janes, R. A. Wycombe Memories. Cabinet Maker 1951 pp. 421-3.

Joel, David. Furniture design set free. 1969.

Joy, Edward. Country life book of chairs. 1968.

Joy, Edward. Furniture. 1972.

Joy, Edward. English Furniture in America in the Georgian Period. Connoisseur, Aug. 1960 pp.68-73.

Joy, Edward. Overseas trade in furniture in the 18th Century. Furniture History vol. 1 1965 pp. 1-10.

Joy, Edward. Overseas trade in furniture in the 19th Century. Furniture History 1970 pp. 62-72.

Kalm, Peter. Visit to England 1748. Translated by Lucas. 1892.

Kingig, Joe. Upholstered Windsors. Antiques, July 1952 pp. 52-3.

Lea, Z. R. The ornamented chair. 1960.

Logie, Gordon. Furniture from machines. 1947.

Longford, Harry. *tape* (High Wycombe P.L.)

Martineau, Harriet. Retrospect of Western travel. 1838.

Massingham, H. J. Men of Earth. 1943.

Mayes, L. J. History of chairmaking in High Wycombe. 1960.

Mayes, L. J. Some customs in the chairmaking trade. Woodworker. Sept. 1960 pp. 175-6; Oct. 1960 pp. 213-5.

Mayes, L. J. The Windsor chairmaker. Woodworker. Mar. 1957 pp. 66-7.

Meader, F. W. Illustrated guide to Shaker furniture. 1972.

Mullet, Bert. 60 years a chairmaker at West Wycombe. 1972. *(notes* High Wycombe P.L.)

Musgrave, Clifford. Queen Mary's Dolls' House. 1972.

North, Leslie. Goodbye to the chair bodgers. Reading Mercury. July 15th 1962.

North, Benjamin. Autobiography of Benjamin North. 1882.

Nutting, Wallace. A Windsor handbook. 1917.

Oliver, J. L. The development and structure of the Furniture industry. 1966.

Ormsbee, T. H. Field guide to Early American furniture. 1951.

Ormsbee, T. H. The Windsor chair. 1962.

Parker Knoll Collection. 1954 *(catalogue)*.

Parnell, William. *see* Sweating Shops Enquiry.

Peate, Iorwerth. Tradition & Folk life: A Welsh view. 1972.

Pevsner, Nikolaus. An enquiry into industrial art in England. 1937.

Plot, Dr. Rober. The natural history of Oxfordshire. 1677.

Porter, G. P. The progress of the Nation. 1836-8.

Roche, Sophia Von la-. Sophia in London 1786. 1933.

Rockell, Samuel. *tape* (High Wycombe P.L.)

Roe, F. G. Victorian furniture. 1952.

Roe, F. G. Windsor chairs. 1953.

Rolph, E. Unemployment Insurance Benefit not paid. N.A.F.T.A. News Dec. 1938.

Rykwert, Joseph *in* Modern chairs 1918-1970.

Shanley, J. R. Will TTT be TNT? F.T.A.T. Record April 1972 pp. 6-7.

Shea, J. G. The American Shakers and their furniture. 1971.

Singleton, Esther. The furniture of our forefathers. 1900.

Skull, Charles E. Fifty years in the Furniture trade. South Bucks Free Press. 8th October 1915.

Snow, G. F. F. Chairs from the Chilterns. Country Life Feb. 6th 1942 pp. 250-251.

South Bucks Free Press. *now* Bucks Free Press.

Sparkes, I. G. Low-back Windsor chairs: Information Sheet No.1 (High Wycombe Museum).

Sparkes, I. G. The Wycombe armchair. Information Sheet No. 2 1972 (High Wycombe Museum)

Steer, F. W. Farm and cottage inventories of Mid Essex. 1950.

Stockwell, David, Windsors in Independence Hall. Antiques. Sept. 1952 pp. 214-5.

Sweating Shops Enquiry: The Select Committee on the Sweating Systems, June 1888.

Symonds, R. W. English cane chairs. Antique Collector. May 1937. pp. 102-106.

Symonds, R. W. The Windsor chair. Apollo. Aug. 1935 pp. 67-71; Nov. 1935 pp. 261-267.

Tayler, A. J. Progress and poverty in Britain 1780-1850. History Vol. XLV 1960.

Thorp, Joseph. An aesthetic conversion. 1912.

Toller Jane. Antique miniature furniture in Great Britain. 1966.

Twiston-Davies, L. *and* Edwards A. Welsh life in the 18th Century. 1939.

Twiston-Davies, L. and Lloyd-Johnes, H. J. Welsh Furniture. 1950.

Victoria & Albert Museum. English chairs. 1970.

Ward, J. D. U. English Windsor Chairs. Antiques. Dec. 1935 pp. 234-7.

Weaver, *Sir* Lawrence. High Wycombe Furniture. 1929.

Whitaker, *Brother* Thomas. A Benedictine-Shaker Link. Unpublished m.s. 1968.

White, J. P. Furniture made at the Pyghtle Works, Bedford. 1901.

White, Sheila. Furniture at his fingertips. Wight Life Feb/Mar. 1973 pp. 13-14 (Albert Lowe)

Williams, Frank. *tape* (High Wycombe P.L.)

Woods, K. S. The rural industries round Oxford. 1921.

Wycombe Chair catalogues and Broadsheets. (High Wycombe P.L.)

Wymer, Norman. English country crafts. 1946.

INDEX